cc:Mail

THE POCKET REFERENCE

cc:Mail

THE POCKET REFERENCE

Christopher Germann

Osborne **McGraw-Hill**

Berkeley New York St. Louis San Francisco
Auckland Bogotá Hamburg London Madrid
Mexico City Milan Montreal New Delhi Panama City
Paris São Paulo Singapore Sydney
Tokyo Toronto

Osborne **McGraw-Hill**
2600 Tenth Street
Berkeley, California 94710
U.S.A.

For information on translations or book distributors outside of the
U.S.A., please write to Osborne **McGraw-Hill** at the above address.

cc:Mail
The Pocket Reference

Publisher: Kenna S. Wood
Aquisitions Editor: William Pollock
Associate Editor: Vicki Van Ausdall
Technical Editor: Kristie Witt
Project Editor: Janis Paris
Copy Editor: Paul Medoff
Proofreader: Linda Medoff
Indexer: Susan DeRenne Coerr
Quality Control Specialist: Bob Myren
Computer Designer: Stefany Otis
Illustrators: Lance Ravella & Susie C. Kim
Cover Design: Bay Graphics Design, Inc.

1234567890 DOC 998765432

ISBN 0-07-881830-3

*To Leigh, Eric, and David; Patty and Dave Germann,
and all other family members who have supported me in
this work, and the experiences that led to it.*

CONTENTS AT A GLANCE

TABLE OF CONTENTS

Acknowledgments

The staff at Osborne/McGraw-Hill has been especially supportive and patient. Bill Pollock, Vicki Van Ausdall, Judy Kleppe, Ann Pharr, Paul Medoff, Janis Paris and others have spent countless hours helping, scolding, laughing, and talking to me on the phone. For all their work I am grateful.

I also wish to thank the people at cc:Mail who have spent their energy and enthusiasm to create a stepping stone to 21st-century communications. Kristie Witt, Jack Marsal, and others have spent much time clarifying numerous details. Special thanks and good luck to Shelley Harrison, who recommended me for this work.

—Christopher Germann

Introduction

If you are like most electronic mail users, you might spend only a few minutes a day reading or writing messages, but your communications are critical to your office productivity. You need to get the most out of your e-mail tool in the least amount of time. I have designed and written this pocket reference specifically for you.

Since cc:Mail's DOS-based package is the foundation for all the other versions (Windows, Macintosh, UNIX), I have written the book to the DOS users, with special comments directed toward the cc:Mail for Windows product. All Windows comments appear at the end of the cc:Mail for DOS comments, and are set apart with a Windows icon that looks like this:

You will find this pocket reference most helpful if you use the Table of Contents and the Index before looking in the body of the text. These tools are complete lists of all the menu items and phrases that you'll encounter on a daily basis. I have further organized the book according to the following outline:

Chapters 1-4   The four major areas of functionality of cc:Mail according to the Main menu in the cc:Mail for DOS software (that is, Read, Prepare, Retrieve, Manage).

Chapters 5-7   Reference material for special features, Macintosh, and troubleshooting.

To make the book easier to use, I have used the following conventions in the text:

| *copy to mailing List* | cc:mail for DOS menu selections are italicized and contain one captalized character highlighted in bold. Use the bolded character for quick selections when the menu appears. |
| **M**essage | cc:Mail for Windows adheres to Windows conventions by offering a quick key for selecting a menu item instead of the mouse. All Windows mnemonics in this book will be represented as a bolded instead of an underlined character. |

Each menu selection in the cc:Mail program is represented in the following format:

Address Message

Notice the headings contain an underlined character instead of bold.

Location: Send menu.

Tells on which menu you may find this selection.

Purpose: To return to the Address menu and add information.

Tells why the menu selection exists.

Step by Step

Contains instructions to use the menu selection.

cc:Mail is the well-known leader in the electronic mail segment of the PC network software industry. Over 10,000 workstations are equipped with cc:Mail software. It has developed into a mature e-mail package with numerous special features that you will likely never come in contact with. But you will always have these tools at your fingertips with this book.

Chapter 1

Reading Messages and Attachments

This chapter discusses the following menu options:

archi**V**e message	**E**rase item
attach new i**T**ems	**F**orward message
c**H**oose another item	**L**ist item titles
c**O**py file item to dos	**M**ove to folder
Copy to folder	**P**rint message
Delete message	repl**Y** to message
display **I**tems	**R**eturn to main menu
display **N**ext message	**W**rite to ascii file

Your cc:Mail program opens with a Main menu offering you several options for receiving, sending, or managing your messages:

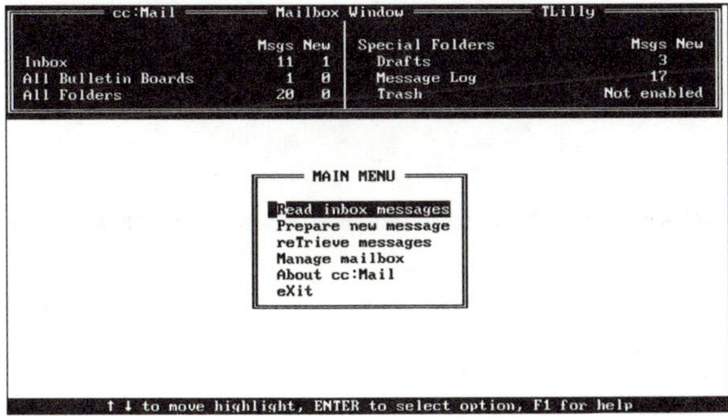

At the Main menu, notice the number of new Inbox messages and the number of total messages in the upper-left corner of the Main menu screen. If you don't have any messages in your Inbox, you will not have a *Read inbox messages* option on the Main menu.

If you don't have any messages and you want to read the messages stored in folders, archive files, or bulletin boards, select *reTrieve messages*. (You will learn about this option in Chapter 4, "Reading and Managing Stored Messages.")

You may use UP ARROW or DOWN ARROW to highlight any of the four messages and select it by pressing ENTER. This chapter covers the first option from the Main menu—the *Read inbox messages* option. With your highlight on this option press ENTER or use the power key *R* to pull up the following Inbox screen:

```
============================ Inbox ============================
  11 JGardner              4/21/92  279t    Conference call to Paris office
  10 PTanner               4/21/92  3777tg   Ad campaign
   9 EBuggs                3/31/92  251t    Meeting on Wednesday
   8 DBernard              3/23/92  222t    Meeting on Friday
   7 JGardner              3/23/92  353t    Travel to New York
   6 JGardner              3/20/92  136t    stuff
   5 JGardner              3/20/92  331t    Thanks
   4 ABarnson              3/20/92  170t    Meeting on Wednesday
   3 PTanner               3/8/92   490t    new products need brochures
   2 ABarnson              3/7/92   518t    Re: Q3 Forecast
   1 ABarnson              3/7/92   149t    Receipt of 3/7/92 11:13AM messa




 ↑ ↓ and ENTER to display message, F5 and F6 to select, Esc to end
```

Read inbox messages (from the Main Menu)

All messages sent or forwarded to you appear in the Inbox Message List. New messages appear in boldface type. Within the Inbox Message List, the message information appears in six different columns with seven categories of data. Information columns include the following:

Inbox Column	Description
Priority	Blank if normal, U for urgent, L for low priority
Message number	Latest messages appear first; to change order refer to Chapter 5, "Special Features"
Sender's name	Name assigned by e-mail administrator
Date sent	Date message was sent
Size of message	In bytes
Type of file attachments (if any)	t = text item, normal cc:Mail message g = graphics file f = file item x = facsimile item (only available with cc:Fax installed)
Subject	First 34 characters

Step by Step

To read your messages in DOS:

1. Use UP ARROW, DOWN ARROW, PGUP, or PGDN to scroll through your list of messages.

2. Highlight the correct message and press ENTER.

➤ *Speed Tip:*   After viewing a mail message, press ENTER or F10 to see the Action menu. The tendency for most users familiar with PC software is to press ESC to go back to the menu. If you press ESC while viewing a message, the Inbox Message List appears, and you must press ENTER again to see the message contents.

 As you start cc:Mail for Windows, the screen will default to the Inbox Message List. Use the pull-down menus to manipulate the messages. You can also use the SmartIcons that appear as small graphics on the screen, shown here:

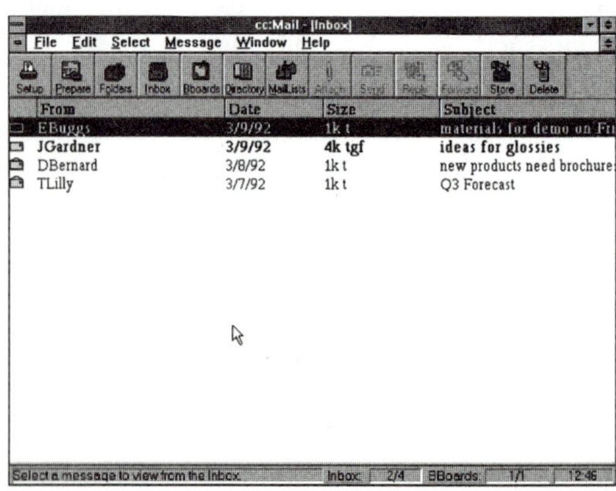

The icon bar at the top of the screen is user
configurable. The columns of information shown in the
Windows Inbox Message List is the same as those
mentioned for the DOS product.

➤ *Speed Tip:*   You can configure cc:Mail for Windows so
that the Inbox appears automatically every time you
enter the program. Select the Windows **File** menu and
click on the Options selection. When the submenu
appears, click on **Display**. You can then fill in several
check boxes that tell the program to automatically start
the Inbox every time you enter the program.

Acting on Your Messages and Attachments

Your cc:Mail messages often have text files, graphics
files, and maybe even fax documents attached to the
main mail message. Messages in cc:Mail fall into two
categories:

- Messages with attachments
- Messages without attachments

The Action menu, used to manipulate your mail
messages, appears after selecting a message from the
Inbox Message List. There are a maximum of 14 options
available on the Action menu, shown next. The options
available on cc:Mail Action menus change according to
which category of message you want to read.

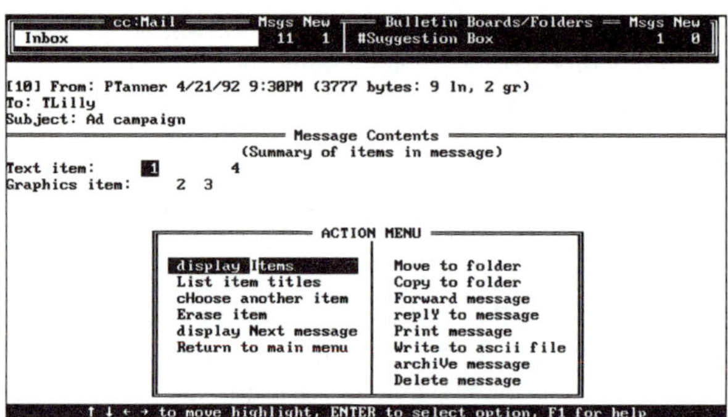

Messages in cc:Mail for Windows are also classified as
messages with attachments or messages without
attachments. From the Inbox, if you click on a message
that does not have any attachments, you will
immediately see the text of the message in the viewer. If
you click on a message with attachments, you will see
an item list (Windows Message screen) with each file
item represented as an icon, as shown below:

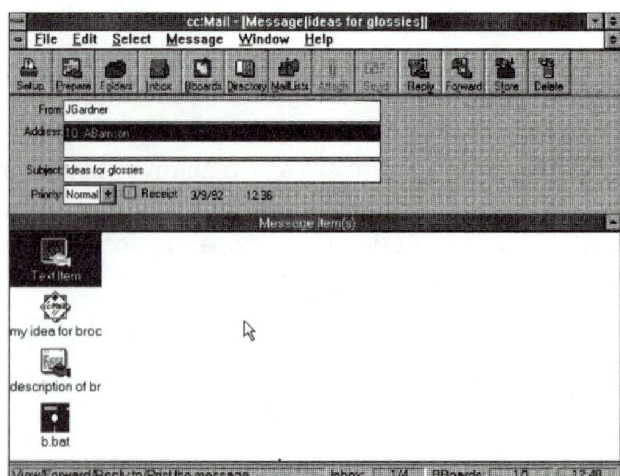

archi_V_e message

Location: Action menu

Purpose: To move a mail message from your Inbox or bulletin board folder to a file on disk. You can store any number of messages in one archive file. When you add a message to an existing archive file, the message is appended. The archive file is a special cc:Mail encrypted file that cannot be read except by cc:Mail.

Use *archiVe message* when you want to save disk space on the network, or when you want to take messages out of your Inbox and folders for safe keeping on diskette. This option appears on the Action menu whether there are message attachments or not.

Step by Step

To archive a message in cc:Mail for DOS:

1. Mark individual messages in the Inbox Message List with F5, or block a group of records by using F5 to begin the block and F6 to end the block.

2. Press ENTER to see the Action menu.

3. Highlight *archiVe message* and press ENTER, or use power key *V* to archive the selected messages.

To archive a message in cc:Mail for Windows:

1. Highlight the message in the Inbox Message List, click on **File** menu, and click on **Store Message**.

2. When the dialog box appears, click on either the Copy or Move button, indicating whether you want to send a copy of the message or the original message.

3. Click on the Archive button and click on OK.

You will then be prompted for a name for the archive file. After you have created one or more archive files, the filenames will appear in the list of archive files.

To archive several nonconsecutive messages at once, click on the messages in your Inbox while holding down the CTRL key. When all desired messages are highlighted, follow the steps that were just outlined. If you want to highlight a list of consecutive messages, you can click and highlight the first message, and then hold down the SHIFT key and click the last message. All the messages between the first and the last will be highlighted. Archive all the messages as outlined above. The group of messages will be appended to your archive file.

attach new iTems

Location: Action menu

Purpose: To associate an external file with an existing mail message. External files, such as graphics or text files, may already exist, or you can create them "on the fly." As you read messages, you can attach new file items to the message before forwarding messages to another person, or before replying to a message.

Step by Step

To attach new items in cc:Mail for DOS:

1. Highlight *attach new iTems* on the Action menu and press ENTER (or press power key *T*).

2. When the Attach menu appears, highlight those types of files that you wish to attach to the message. It's the same Attach menu as when you prepare original messages, as discussed in Chapter 2.

 To attach a new message in cc:Mail for Windows:

When the message is highlighted in the Inbox, the Attach icon, represented as a paper clip, is grayed-out (not usable). You must first click on the Select menu and then on **Forward** message. When the message "Forward as new?" appears, click on OK. You are then in the message preparation mode, and the Attach icon will be available. If you are not using SmartIcons, click the **Message** menu and click on Attach, as described in Chapter 2.

➤ *Speed Tip:*   When using Windows, you can click and drag a file item icon to another window so you can attach it to a new message. You can also drag the icon to a bulletin board or folder for storage.

cHoose another item

Location: Action menu

Purpose: to select a file item for viewing. This option only appears on the Action menu after you have viewed a message with attachments. After choosing this option, you can perform actions such as display, erase, move, copy, etc.

Step by Step

To choose another item in cc:Mail for DOS:

1. Highlight *cHoose another item* on the Action menu and press ENTER, or use power key *H*.

2. Use the arrow keys to move the highlight cursor to the desired item in the Item title list.

3. Press ENTER, and the number item will be highlighted as the Action menu reappears.

You may be frustrated by the steps necessary to view your next file item. Return to the Action menu; the usual sequence of events is to select *cHoose another item* and then select *dIsplay item* to actually see the attachment. The Summary of Items in Message screen is presented below.

Summary of Items in Message screen

```
From: TLilly 4/21/92 9:39PM (3753 bytes: 9 In, 2 gr)
To:
Subject: Ad campaign
                            ===== Message Contents =====
                         (Summary of items in message)
Text item:        1          4
Graphics item:       2  3

Item title   1: main mail message
             2: Idea for 4-color glossy
             3: two color graphic
             4: text description of two graphics files




     ↑ ↓ ← → to move highlight, ENTER to select item, Esc to cancel
```

cOpy file item to dos

Location: Action menu

Purpose: To move a copy of a message attachment to
disk. This option only appears on the Action menu when
there are file or graphics items attached to a mail message.

Step by Step

To copy a file item to cc:Mail for DOS:

1. Highlight a specific file item by using *cHoose
   another item* on the Action menu and press ENTER,
   or press power key *H*.

2. The Action menu will appear when the file item is
   highlighted.

3. Highlight *cOpy file item to dos* and press ENTER, or
   press power key *O*.

To copy a file item to DOS from cc:Mail for Windows:

To copy or move a file item to DOS from Windows,
highlight the message and click on the **File** menu. Click
on **Save** or Save **As** to name the item.

Copy to folder

Location: Action menu

Purpose: To make a copy of the currently displayed
message in a storage folder. The folder may exist
already, or may be created as you copy the message.

Copy to folder leaves the original message in your Inbox and creates a copy of the message in the folder. This is useful for copying the message to a personal storage folder or to a public bulletin board that is accessed by a group of people.

Step by Step

To copy an item to a folder in cc:Mail for DOS:

1. Highlight *Copy to folder* and press ENTER, or press power key *C*. The list of folders appears on the screen. The bulletin board folders available to everyone on the network are marked with a crosshatch (#).

2. Use the arrow keys to highlight the name of the folder, or begin typing the name of the folder at the prompt that appears on the screen and press ENTER. The current message will be copied to the folder.

To copy a file item to a folder in cc:Mail for Windows:

1. Highlight the message in the Inbox.

2. Click on the **F**ile menu.

3. Click on **S**tore Message.

4. Click on the Copy button from the Store Message dialog box.

5. Click the Folder button and click on OK. If a list of folders already exists, click on a folder name and the highlighted message will be copied to the folder. If no folder exists, fill in a name for the new folder and click OK. The message will be copied to the new folder.

Delete message

Location: Action menu

Purpose: To remove the currently displayed message and all its attachments from all message lists. If the message exists in the Inbox, but there are copies in folders or bulletin boards, the message will be removed from all storage locations.

Delete message removes the entire message with all of its attachments. This option differs from *Erase item*, which only deletes items that are attached to a message (this option only appears onscreen if a message has attachments). You will be asked to confirm your decision to remove the selected message.

 To delete a mail message from the Inbox in cc:Mail for Windows, highlight the message and press DEL.

display Items

Location: Action menu

Purpose: To display a highlighted message item listed in the Summary of Items in Message screen. If a message does not have attachments, use *display Item* to review the text of a message. If a message has attachments, you will have to use the option *cHoose another item* to highlight an item, and then use *display Item*.

To display the contents of a file item in cc:Mail for Windows, double-click the icon (for text items), use SHIFT

+ double-click (if items are more complex, like graphics), or click the **M**essage menu (shown earlier in the chapter) and click **V**iew item. cc:Mail tries to open the item, whether it be graphics, text, or a file, using special viewing filters. There are several filters available for popular file formats such as Lotus graphics, TIFF, and WordPerfect. (See Chapter 5, "Special Features," which discusses other applications.) The Message window appears.

display <u>N</u>ext message

Location: Action menu

Purpose: To highlight the next message shown in the Inbox Message List or to display the next message of a selected group of items.

As you are reading through your messages, you can mark individual messages that you want to review. You can also highlight a group of consecutive messages and review them one at a time without going back to the Inbox Message List.

Step by Step

To display a group of messages in cc:Mail for DOS:

1. From your Inbox, press F5 as many times as you need to mark individual files, or press F5 to begin a block of selected files and F6 to end the block.

2. Press ENTER to see the Action menu (this particular Action menu appears only when you are dealing with a group of messages).

3. Highlight *display **A**ll messages* and press ENTER, or use power key **A**, to see the first message that you marked. Highlight *display **N**ext message* and press ENTER, or use power key **N** to see the next message in the group that you marked.

4. Press F10 or ESC to see the Action menu. To unmark messages, highlight each message individually and press F5, or unmark all messages at once by pressing ESC.

Erase item

Location: Action menu

Purpose: To delete a message attachment.

Use the *c**H**oose another item* option to highlight one item in the list of attachments and when the Action menu reappears, highlight **Erase item** and press ENTER. You will be asked to confirm your decision to delete the selected item.

Forward message

Location: Action menu

Purpose: To send the currently displayed message to another person or an entire group.

If you wish to show the original author on the message heading, do not modify the message before you address it. When you forward a message, the original message heading is located beneath the new heading. The two headings are separated by a dashed line. A new heading is added to the message every time it gets forwarded. This is useful for tracking a message that gets forwarded by several people.

If you make changes to the original message, the heading on the dashed line reads "Forwarded with Changes."

To forward a message in cc:Mail for Windows:

After reading a message (you must open the message for reading before you can forward it), you may forward it as a new message.

1. Click the **Message** menu, then click on the Forward option or the Forward SmartIcon.

2. You may then address and send the message as if you were sending a new message, as described in Chapter 2, "Sending Messages and Attachments." Fill out the message header by selecting an addressee and a subject.

3. Click the Send SmartIcon, or click the **Message** menu and click **Send**.

List item titles

Location: Action menu

Purpose: To display a list of all the text, file, or graphics items attached to the message. This option only appears on the Action menu when you select a message with attachments.

Some item titles may not appear because the titles are optional. After viewing the list, you may change the order of attachments. You might want to change the order before forwarding the message to another person.

Step by Step

To change the order of item titles in cc:Mail for DOS:

1. Press F5 to mark the attachment (a pointer will appear next to the message).

2. Use the arrow keys to move the pointer to the new location in the list.

3. Press ALT-F5 to move the item, or press ALT-F6 to copy the item to the new location.

4. Press F10 to restore the Action menu to the screen.

<u>M</u>ove to folder

Location: Action menu

Purpose: To relocate the currently displayed message to an existing storage folder or to a folder that you create as you move the message.

When you select the *Move to folder* option in cc:Mail for DOS, you will see a list of folders that only belong to you and bulletin boards that are common to everyone on the network (marked with a #). Highlight the desired folder and the message file will be inserted automatically, similar to the process described in the *Copy to folder* section, except the message is moved, not duplicated.

To move a mail message or file item to a folder in cc:Mail for Windows:

1. Highlight the message in the Inbox.

2. Click on the **F**ile menu and click on Store Message.

3. Click on the Move button from the Store Message dialog box.

4. Click the Folder button and click on OK. As the window containing the list of folders appears, click on a folder name where you want to move the message. To create a folder while looking at your list of folders, you must click the **F**ile menu and select **C**reate. You cannot create a folder while moving a file to it, as you can in the DOS product.

Print message

Location: Action menu

Purpose: To print a message on a local or network printer. There are two ways to print a message. You may use the *Print message* option on the Action menu after you view the message, or while viewing the message you can press the specially assigned function key F8.

Step by Step

To print a message in cc:Mail for DOS:

1. Press F5 at the beginning of the block.

2. Move the cursor to the end of the block and press F6.

➤ *Speed Tip:* If you have a printer connected directly to your computer, take a few minutes to set your e-mail printing configuration. This is especially important when you need to print graphics or fax attachments. To set up the correct printer, return to the Main menu and select *Manage mailbox*. Then, from the Manage menu, select *Change profile*. In the *Profile menu*, select the *change printer Type* option. You will then see several options relating to printer types. Choose the appropriate option and press ENTER. The default option refers to the printer already chosen by your network system administrator.

To print a message in cc:Mail for Windows:

To send a message item to a printer in cc:Mail for Windows, click the Print icon button, or click the **File** menu and click **Print**.

replY to message

Location: Action menu

Purpose: To respond to a message by adding additional comments, a new message, or additional file items. Use *replY to message* so that you don't have to go all the way back to the Main menu and start with *Prepare new message*.

Step by Step

To reply to a message in cc:Mail for DOS:

1. Highlight *replY to message* on the Action menu and press ENTER, or press power key **Y**. A blank message area will appear where you can type in your reply message. The header will already by filled out with the same subject line.

2. Press F10 after typing the message. The Send Action menu appears with various options associated with sending messages. These are described in greater detail in Chapter 2.

Sometimes you may want to include the original message in your reply so the receiver can use it as a reference. When you want to reply by including the original message:

1. Start editing the message as you read it. For example, begin editing by pressing DOWN ARROW.

2. Once you have typed a new message or edited the original message, press F10, and the Address menu will appear.

3. Change the list of addresses if desired.

4. Highlight *repl**Y** to sender* and press ENTER, or use power key **Y**.

5. When the Send menu appears, attach new items if desired, highlight **Send** *message* and press ENTER, or use power key **S**.

In version 4.0, cc:Mail will automatically insert the text "Re:" to the beginning of each subject line of a reply message. This enhancement will help you determine at a glance as you look in your Inbox which messages are replies.

 To reply to a message in cc:Mail for Windows:

1. Read the message first by clicking on the highlighted message in the Inbox Message List.

2. Click on the Reply SmartIcon, or click **Message**, or use keystroke combination ALT-Y.

3. The Reply dialog box will appear. Choose whether
   to retain original addressee (keep the same
   addresses on the address list) and whether to keep
   all original message items. Click OK.

4. Send the message using normal send procedures,
   discussed in Chapter 2.

<u>R</u>eturn to main menu

Location: Action menu

Purpose: To cancel current operations and display the
Main menu. Choose the option by highlighting *Return to
main menu* and pressing ENTER or pressing the power
key *R*.

<u>W</u>rite to ascii file

Location: Action menu

Purpose: To copy the contents of the currently selected
message to an ASCII text file. You will be prompted to
fill in the name of the file to which the message will be
copied.

Step by Step

To write a message to an ASCII file in cc:Mail for DOS:

1. After selecting the file, choose *Write to ascii file*.

You can save a Windows mail message in Windows (ANSI) format or you can save it in a DOS-equivalent format.

1. Highlight the message in the Inbox.

2. Click on the **F**ile menu and then click on Save **A**s.

3. At the bottom of the Save As dialog box, make sure the Windows (ANSI) format box is checked if you will use the text file in Windows. If you will use the file in DOS, uncheck this box.

4. Type in the correct path and filename and click OK.

Chapter 2

Sending Messages and Attachments

This chapter will discuss the following commands:

Address message	*copy to mailing List*
address to bboard/Folder	*Copy to person*
address to Mailing list	*display Message*
Address to person	*edit sUbject*
attach bboard/folder Msgs	*eNd addressing*
attach copy of dos File	*eNd attaching*
attach Graphics item	*reQuest receipt*
attach Snapshots	*Return to main menu*
attach Text item	*Send message*
Blind copy to person	*set Priority level*

In this chapter, you will learn how to address, create, attach items to, and send a message.

You will become familiar with sending cc:Mail messages if you divide the process into four steps:

- addressing a message
- writing a message in the Text Editor
- attaching file items to a message (optional)
- using the mailing lists

If you don't send any files along with the mail message, there are only three stages of sending a message.

There are several menus that you will use to send a message. All of the quick reference entries in this chapter appear in either the Address, Send, or Attach menu. To see how the menus are used together, refer to Figure A-2 in Appendix A.

Your cc:Mail program opens with the Main menu. To address, attach items to, or send a message, select *Prepare new message* from the Main menu.

Prepare new message

To begin the process of addressing, creating, attaching items to, or sending a message, highlight *Prepare new message* from the Main menu and press ENTER, or use power key *P*. The Address menu appears with ten options. Notice the message addressing information at the top of the screen. cc:Mail automatically fills out the "From:" line at the top of the page with your name and immediately highlights the *Address to person* option on the Address menu. The other options on the Address menu help you to fill the header with addressing information.

In cc:Mail for Windows, message preparation follows the DOS product closely. The graphical user interface (GUI) in Windows, however, allows several shortcuts. For example, you can fill out the address message header by clicking on either the directory or a private mailing list and then selecting a name from the list.

Address message

Location: Send menu

Purpose: To return to the Address menu and add appropriate information to the message header listed at the top of the screen. You will usually address a message immediately after you select *Prepare new message* from the Main menu. However, this selection appears on the Send menu so you can change your addressing information before you send the message.

You will sometimes begin sending a message by including files or typing a message before addressing the message. You have the flexibility in cc:Mail to create and send a message in the order that you want to do it. The message must have at least one person/bboard/folder listed on the "To:" line of the message header or the message will not be sent.

Step by Step

To add or change address information once you are in the Send menu in cc:Mail for DOS:

1. Highlight *Address message* in the Send menu and press ENTER, or use the power key **A**. The Address menu will appear with all normal addressing options.

2. Add names and/or mailing lists to the address portion of the message header by selecting the appropriate Address menu option.

3. Highlight *eNd addressing* and press ENTER to finish addressing and return to the Send menu.

In cc:Mail for Windows, you can address your message at any time by clicking on the Address button in the message header. Then select the appropriate addressing option (person, mailing list, bulletin board, or folder).

address to bboard/Folder

Location: Address menu

Purpose: To send messages directly to a public bulletin board area on the network or to a storage folder.

You will often want to store the message you send in a location where others may reference the information on a system bulletin board, or to a storage folder, where you can keep a private collection of all the messages you send. You can create a new folder as you address your message.

Step by Step

To send a message to a bulletin board or storage folder in cc:Mail for DOS:

1. Highlight the *address to bboard/**F**older* option on the Address menu and press ENTER, or use the power key **F**.

2. To create a new folder, type the name of the folder on the prompt line and press ENTER. The new folder name will appear on the list of folders every time you send a message.

3. Highlight the desired folder name and press ENTER. A "To folder:" line will appear in the address portion

of the message, followed by the name of the folder
you selected.

To address the message to a bulletin board, folder, or
mailing list in cc:Mail for Windows:

1. Click on the Send icon, or click on the **S**elect
   pull-down menu and then click on **P**repare Message.

2. When the new message window appears, click on
   the Address button to the left of the message
   header, or click on the **M**essage pull-down menu,
   and then click on **A**ddress.

3. When the Address Message window appears, look
   at the "**S**elect From" box to the left of the directory.
   Click on either Mail **L**ist, Pri**v** MList, **B**Board, or
   Folder.

4. Click on the appropriate list or folder from the
   window that appears.

➤ *Speed Tip:* If your cc:Mail/network administrator has
activated the Message Log feature, you can create a
new folder called Message Log, and a copy of all your
outgoing messages will automatically be saved there.

address to <u>M</u>ailing list

Location: Address menu

Purpose: To send a message to a list of people who are
included on a mailing list that has been created. Instead
of adding several individuals one at a time to your
message header, create a mailing list and cc:Mail will
automatically send the message to everyone on the list.

Step by Step

To send a message to a mailing list in cc:Mail for DOS:

1. Highlight *address to **M**ailing list* on the Address menu and press ENTER, or use the power key **M**. The list of mailing lists available to you appears in a display window at the top of the screen.

2. Use the arrow keys to highlight a selection and press ENTER, or type the name of the mailing list directly on the prompt line that appears in the Message Contents area.

➤ *Speed Tip:* You don't have to create a mailing list beforehand. You can create a list as you address and send your message. Follow steps 3 and 4 below.

3. Instead of highlighting an existing name, type a new name for a mailing list at the prompt line.

4. Then choose names from the cc:Mail directory. Each name you choose will be added to the new mailing list. The mailing list will appear on your list of mailing lists every time you send a message. The mailing list you create will only be available to you, not to everyone on the network. Only the administrator can create public mailing lists.

To address a message to a public or private mailing list in cc:Mail for Windows, click on **Priv** MList or MList in the Address Message window. Then select the name of the list from the window that appears.

Address to person

Location: Address menu

Purpose: To select one or more persons to whom you will send the message. You can add as many people to the address list as you want. The Address menu is shown here:

➤ *Speed Tip:*   If you routinely send a message to the same group of people, you can speed up the addressing by using a mailing list. Highlight the addre*ss to **M**ailing list* option on the Address menu to select a public mailing list (marked with a #) or create your own list by typing the name of the list and adding names from the directory.

Step by Step

To address a message in cc:Mail for DOS:

1. Highlight *Address to person* in the Address menu and press ENTER, or use the power key *A*.

2. When the directory of names appears, highlight a name and press ENTER.

3. Repeat this procedure for each person you want to add to the address list. You can have individual

people on your address list along with public and/or private mailing lists as shown below:

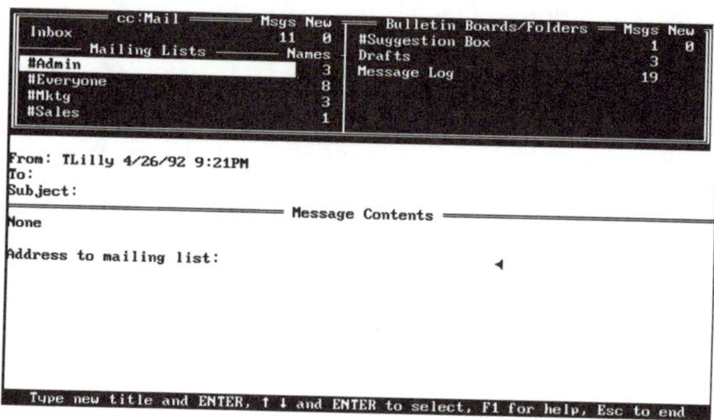

In cc:Mail for Windows, the cc:Mail directory automatically appears in the Address Message window as you begin addressing the message. In the directory, notice the icon to the left of each name in the list. The mailbox icon shows that the person is local, and the phone icon shows that the person is remote.

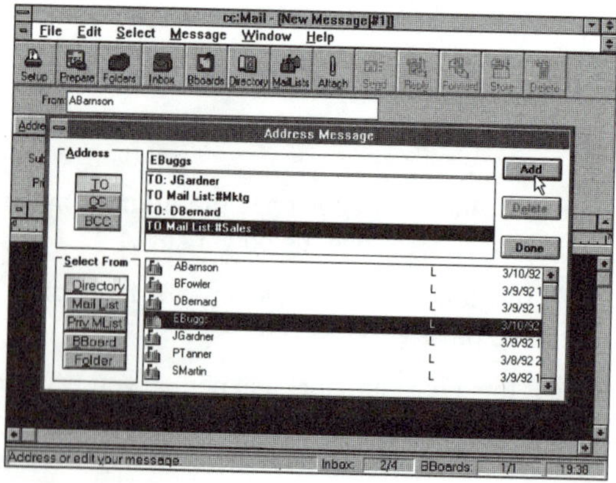

To address a message in cc:Mail for Windows:

1. Click on the Prepare message icon, or choose the **S**elect menu and click the **P**repare Message option.

2. When the Address Message dialog box appears, fill out the addressee by typing a name or clicking on a name in the directory. When the name is highlighted, click the Add button, double-click on the name, or press ENTER.

3. Fill out the other addressing options (copy to a person or list, blind copy to a person or list, request a receipt, set the priority). Click on Done.

➤ *Speed Tip:* Sometimes when you send a message, you will use several windows to correctly address, write, and attach items to the mail message. You can use the Options submenus from the **F**ile menu to select where you want to start preparing the message. Your choices are the Address Message window, the Text Editor, the Subject line of the message header, or the Attach dialog box. Select **O**ptions from the **F**ile menu, then click on **M**essage to see the message preparation submenu. Then select your choice from the "Start Messages In:" section of the dialog window.

attach bboard/folder <u>M</u>sgs

Location: Attach menu

Purpose: To attach stored messages as file items to a newly created message. Often you will want to refer to a message from your private storage folders or the public

bulletin board when you communicate with coworkers.
Use this option to attach the message for reference.

Step by Step

To attach a stored message in cc:Mail for DOS:

1. From the Attach menu, highlight *attach
    bboard/folder Msgs* and press ENTER (or use power
    key *M*).

2. Highlight the desired name of the folder and/or
    bulletin board and press ENTER.

3. You will see a list of messages similar to your Inbox
    or a prompt line where you can enter the number of
    the appropriate message. Highlight a message or fill
    in the message number and press ENTER. A new
    item number will appear on the file item screen. The
    "Subject:" line of the attached message will appear
    as the file item's title.

You will then be able to make another selection from the
Attach menu, shown here.

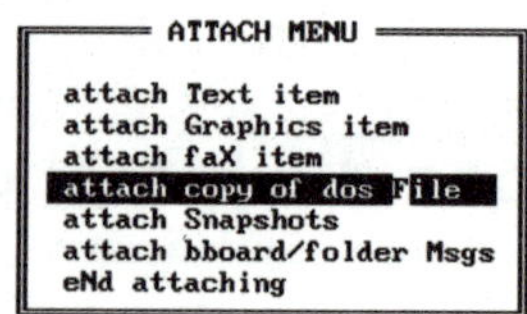

You can attach up to 19 file items to any one mail
message for a total of 20 items. (You can add 20 items if
you don't include message text when you send the
original message—that is, send only attachments.)

attach copy of dos File

Location: Attach menu, Send menu

Purpose: To attach and send any type of disk file (up to a limit of 20).

If, for example, you have drafted a document in your favorite word processor and you don't want to type the information over again in a mail message, you can simply include the file with a short mail message telling the recipient what kind of file you have attached.

Step by Step

To attach a DOS file to your message in cc:Mail for DOS:

1. Highlight *attach copy of dos **F**ile* from the Send or the Attach menu and press ENTER, or use power key **F**.

2. The menu will go away and you will see a list of files in the current DOS directory. Use arrow keys to move through the list of files and press ENTER on the selected file, or type the correct path and filename on the prompt line and press ENTER.

You do not have to know the filename. You can use DOS wildcard characters (* for many characters and ? for one character) to narrow a search. After attaching a file, the list of files will go away, and you will see a new item number appear in the file item list above the Attach menu. The filename and creation date will appear as the title of the file item.

To attach a copy of a DOS file in cc:mail for Windows:

1. While creating a new message, click on the Attach icon, or click on the **M**essage pull-down menu, and then click on Attach. The Message Item Attachment screen appears as shown in the "attach new i**T**ems" section of this chapter.

2. Fill in the filename or change directories and then enter the filename. Click OK.

3. If you need to create a file to attach, click on the appropriate icon button at the bottom of the window (i.e., Text, Text-Editor, Grx-Editor, or Apps). You can also create a file in another application. For more information on how to "launch" other applications, see Chapter 5, "Special Features."

attach Graphics item

Location: Attach menu

Purpose: To include a graphics picture created with cc:Mail's graphics drawing utility program.

As soon as you select this option, the graphics drawing screen appears with menus on the bottom and right sides of the screen. You can draw a graphics image using the tools provided in the menus (attaching graphics items that you draw as you attach them). The following list briefly describes the commands to use within the graphics utility:

Graphics Command	Keystroke
Help	F1
Display and Remove graphics menus	F9
Finish drawing, return to message	F10
Move the cursor around the drawing	Arrow keys
Select tool	Power keys, or move selection box around menus and press ENTER
Freehand, thin lines	F
Freehand, thick lines	R
Empty circles	C
Solid circles	I
Empty boxes	B
Solid boxes	O
Straight line, thin	L
Straight line, thick	T
Small lettering	A
Large lettering	Z
Display spacing grid	G
Move a rectangular part of screen	M
Begin using selected tool	ENTER
End using selected tool	ENTER

Step by Step

To attach a graphics item created with the graphics
utility from cc:Mail for DOS:

1. Select *attach **G**raphics item* from the Attach menu.

2. Create the picture in the graphics screen that
    appears.

3. When you finish the drawing, press F10 to close the
    graphics screen and immediately return to the
    Attach menu. The new graphics item will appear as
    a file item attachment on the screen.

 cc:Mail for Windows employs the Windows Paintbrush
application to create graphics images.

To attach a graphics item:

1. Click on the Attach icon.

2. Click on the Graphics Editor button in the list of file
    item attachments at the bottom of the File Item
    Attachment dialog box.

3. Create the drawing in the Paintbrush application
    and save the file using the file and directory
    settings.

4. When the new graphics file appears in the file list,
    double-click on the filename. The message file item
    list will appear, showing an icon of each item
    attached to the current message.

attach new items

Location: Send menu

Purpose: To attach graphics files, text files, or DOS files to the message you are about to send.

Step by Step

To attach file items to a mail message in cc:Mail for DOS:

1. From the Send menu, highlight *attach new iTems* and press ENTER, or use power key *T*.

2. When the Attach menu appears, highlight the type of item you wish to attach and press ENTER, or use the appropriate power key.

3. After attaching all items you desire, highlight *eNd attaching* from the Attach menu and press ENTER or use power key *N*. You will then return to the Send menu again.

In cc:Mail for Windows, to attach any sort of file to the mail message, click on the Attach icon, or select the **M**essage menu and then the Attach option. The Message Item Attachment dialog box is shown here.

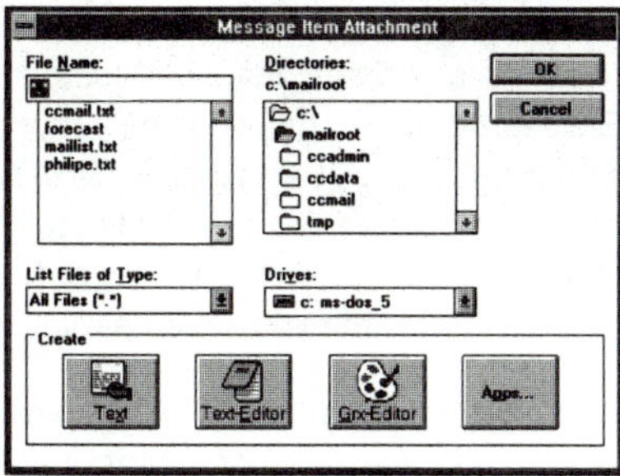

▶ *Speed Tip:* In cc:Mail for Windows, you can attach a portion of another document from another currently running application by using the Windows clipboard.

To attach an item from the Windows clipboard in a
cc:Mail for Windows message:

1. Choose the standard Windows Copy command in
   any Windows application to place the item in the
   clipboard.

2. Switch to cc:Mail for Windows.

3. Type a new message in the Text Item window.

4. Close the Text Item Window so the Message Item
   window is displayed.

5. Click the Paste icon, or click on the **E**dit menu and
   then click on the **P**aste option.

6. Fill out the name of the attachment in the Attach
   Prefix dialog box. The clipboard item will be
   attached to your message for mailing.

attach Snapshots

Location: Attach menu

Purpose: To attach a cc:Mail "snapshot" (screen capture)
file from a DOS directory to the message you will send.
This action operates just like attaching a DOS file. You
will be prompted to select a file from the default DOS
directory, or you can change the directory to find the
snapshot screen capture file you saved earlier.

Use the utility program SNAPSHOT.COM to make a
screen capture of an important document or anything
you are working on. For example, when cc:Mail can't
read a Lotus or WordPerfect file, you can use this screen

capture utility to attach a graph or other interesting item to you mail messages. Chapter 5, "Special Features," describes SNAPSHOT.COM.

attach Text item

Location: Attach menu

Purpose: To include another text message with the original message item.

Use this option to attach a text file that the recipient may use separately from the original mail message. If you type the information in the mail message, the recipient has the additional step of copying the mail message to a DOS text file.

Step by Step

To attach a text item to a mail message in cc:Mail for DOS:

1. After addressing a message, while you are looking at the Send menu, highlight *attach new Items* and press ENTER, or use the power key *T*.

2. When the Attach menu appears, highlight *attach Text items* and press ENTER or use power key *T*.

3. When a blank text editor screen appears, type your text item and press F10 to finish.

4. Fill in the "item title" (optional) and press ENTER to return to the Attach menu. You can attach more file items, or choose *eNd attaching* to return to the Send menu.

Blind copy to person

Location: Address menu

Purpose: To send a copy of a message to a third party without the original recipient(s) of your message knowing that the message was sent to someone else.

In cc:Mail for DOS, this option works exactly the same way that *Copy to person* works. Highlight the option and press ENTER, or use power key *B*. Then select the names on the list that will receive a blind copy and press ENTER.

In cc:Mail for Windows, while filling in the address in the message header, click on BCC and select a person's name from the mailing directory that appears in the window below.

blind copy to list

Location: Address menu

Purpose: To send a copy of a message to all the people on a mailing list without the original recipient(s) knowing that the message was sent to someone else.

Step by Step

To send a blind copy of a message to a list of people with cc:Mail for DOS:

1. Select *blind copy to list* from the Address menu. cc:Mail will display the mailing list window (the

same window that appears if you choose *address to Mailing list*) with a prompt underneath it.

2. Select an existing list, or enter the name of a new list and add names to create it. In both cases, the names will appear in the address header on the line beginning with "bcc:"

cc:Mail for Windows also offers a blind copy to list option from the Address Message dialog box. Click on the BCC button and then click on either the Mail **L**ist or Pri**v** MList button. Then as you select a mailing list, all of the names in the list will appear with a BCC label in the address header.

copy to mailing List

Location: Address menu

Purpose: To send a message to a predefined list of people. Use this option to send a message to a commonly identified group of people, such as a marketing or sales department.

Step by Step

To send a message to everyone on a mailing list (or to create your own mailing list) in cc:Mail for DOS:

1. Highlight *copy to mailing List* in the Address menu and press ENTER, or use power key *L*.

2. A list of public and private mailing lists appears on the screen. The public lists available to everyone on the network have a # preceding the name of the list.

Highlight the target list and press ENTER, or, on the prompt line, type the name of a new list (for example, administration, sales, or weekly staff meeting attendees) and press ENTER.

3. The cc:Mail directory appears on the screen. Highlight each name you wish to add to your mailing list and press ENTER. Repeat this process for everyone you wish to add.

4. Press F10 or ESC to finish creating your list.

5. Highlight the new list on the list of mailing lists and press ENTER. The name of the mailing list appears in the message header, and your message will be sent to each member of the list. If you select *reQuest receipt* for the message, you will receive a receipt message from everyone on the list who reads the message.

In cc:Mail for Windows, you can begin filling out the message header by typing or clicking on appropriate buttons. To address a copy to a mailing list click Mail List or Pri**v** MList and begin typing the names, or, when the mailing list appears in a window, click on the name of the mailing list.

Copy to person

Location: Address menu

Purpose: To send your mail message to an interested third party. cc:Mail sends the message as a regular mail message except for adding a line with a "cc:" and the names of others receiving a copy of the message in the message header.

Step by Step

To send a copy to a person in cc:Mail for DOS:

1. From the Address menu, highlight *Copy to person* and press ENTER, or use power key *C*.

2. The cc:Mail directory of everyone on your cc:Mail system appears on the screen. Type the first few letters of the copy recipient, or use the arrow keys to highlight the person. Press ENTER.

 In cc:Mail for Windows, you can begin filling out the message header by typing or clicking on appropriate buttons. To address a copy to a person click **CC** and begin typing the name or select the names from the directory.

display <u>M</u>essage

Location: Send menu

Purpose: To display on the screen the mail message that will be sent.

Use this option when you need to change the contents of the message at the last minute, or if you need to refer to the text of the message for another reason. This option does not appear in the Send menu if you haven't already typed a text message.

Step by Step

To display a message on the screen so you can make changes before sending it in cc:Mail for DOS.

1. From the Send menu, highlight *display Message* and press ENTER or use power key **M**.

2. When the message appears in the text editor, make changes as desired.

3. Press F10 to finish editing the message. The Send menu will appear again so you can send the message after editing.

edit sUbject

Location: Send menu

Purpose: To return to the message header of the current message and change what is entered on the "Subject:" line of the message header.

In cc:Mail for DOS, select this option from the Send menu to either add a subject line for the first time or to change what you entered previously in the subject line.

In cc:Mail for Windows, you can return to the subject at any time just by clicking on the "Subject:" line of the addressing information with the mouse.

eNd addressing

Location: Address menu

Purpose: To complete the addressing of a mail message and begin typing your message. You can use *eNd addressing* if you want to type the subject and/or the message text first. You will have a chance later (in the Send menu) to change the addressing before you actually send the message.

Step by Step

To exit the address stage in cc:Mail for DOS:

1. Add the individuals, bulletin boards, or folders that will receive your message to the message header (see *address to bboard/Folder*).

2. Highlight *eNd addressing* in the Address menu and press ENTER, or use power key *N*. The Address menu will disappear, and the cursor will move to the "Subject:" line of the message header.

3. Enter a subject line and press ENTER to enter the Text Editor and begin typing the message.

To finish addressing a message in cc:Mail for Windows, click the Done button in the Addressing dialog box.

Text Editor

The cc:Mail text editor appears on the screen after you select *eNd addressing* from the Address menu.

```
From: TLilly 4/26/92 6:16PM (362 bytes: 9 ln)
To: ABarnson
Subject: Proposal
============================ Message Contents ============================
      Alison:

      Please review the attached file (it's in our word processing
      format) and tell me what you think. I will use this material
      in our proposal for the the Johnson account.

      Thanks,

      Tim




Window:   1 - 24   Lines:  13    Edit: ↑ ↓ ← →         Help: F1       End: ENTER
```

The text editor is a functional word processor that has several unique features. New to version 4.0, cc:Mail provides keyboard definition files from some of the most popular word processors. This will save you time and frustration learning new keystrokes (see "Importing keystroke definition files" in Chapter 5).

➤ *Speed Tip:*   Press the INSERT key to switch into Insert mode before typing your message. You will feel like you are in what's normally the default typing mode in most word processors. The Text Editor provides two editing modes to write messages. Edit mode is just like a common typeover mode in word processors. Insert mode allows you to use the arrow keys and type anywhere in the message without typing over any character. Edit mode is the default mode.

Text Editor Keystroke Reference

Desired Action	*Keystroke*
Help	F1
End editing	F10
Cancel message	F10, R
Cursor keys	
Move to upper-left corner of screen	HOME
Move to end of line	END
Move right one character	RIGHT ARROW
Move left one character	LEFT ARROW
Move to beginning of line	F3 once
Move to end of line	F3 twice
Move to next tab stop	TAB
Move to previous tab stop	SHIFT-TAB
Scroll text down 1/2 screen (12 lines)	PGDN

Text Editor Keystroke Reference (*continued*)

Desired Action	*Keystroke*
Scroll text up 1/2 screen (12 lines)	PGUP
Scroll text down 1 full screen	CTRL-PGDN
Scroll text up 1 full screen	CTRL-PGUP
Move to beginning of text	CTRL-HOME
Move to end of text	CTRL-END
Edit mode (overwrites characters)	INSERT (toggle)
Insert mode (moves characters	INSERT (toggle)
Insert blank line	ALT-F3
Delete one character at cursor	DEL
Delete one character back	BACKSPACE
Delete from cursor to end of line (the entire line that contains markers will be deleted regardless of where the marker exists in the line)	ALT-F4
Mark beginning of block	F5
Mark end of block	F6
Delete a block (mark with F5, F6)	ALT-F4
Search for text	F7
(F7 to repeat the same search)	
Delete search phrase (F7 to search)	ALT-F4
Search and replace text	ALT-F7
Change margin settings	F4
Restore formatting (margins) (mark text, place cursor in block)	ALT-F8
Move a block (mark text with F5, F6)	ALT-F8
Copy a block (mark text with F5, F6)	ALT-F6
Clear block markers	ESC

Text Editor Keystroke Reference (*continued*)

Desired Action	Keystroke
Mark a single line as a block	F5
Change screen colors	ALT-F1
Color highlight word (First select color combination with ALT-F1)	F2
Color highlight block (use F5, F6)	ALT-F2
Import DOS ASCII file	ALT-F9
Write to ASCII file (block F5, F6)	F9
Print entire message	F8
Print block (block with F5, F6)	F8

The cc:Mail for Windows Text Editor uses standard Microsoft Windows editing keys. Using a mouse to do such things as selecting (blocking), copying, and pasting to other messages is most advantageous. The text editor in cc:Mail for Windows adds three special features that you might find helpful.

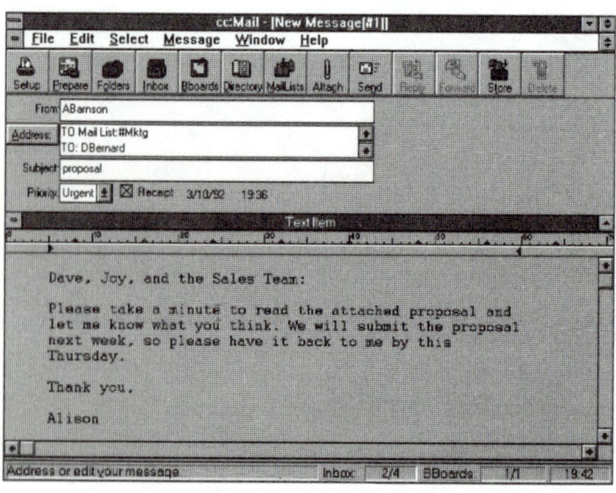

Highlighting Text   You can highlight all or any part of text with the color palette.

1. Select the text to highlight.

2. Click the Highlighting icon button; press the right mouse button (left mouse button for left-handed mice); or click on the **Edit** menu, the Text Editor option, and finally the Color **H**ighlighting option from the submenu.

3. Make the color selections as provided in the Color Highlighting dialog box. Click OK.

Changing Margins and Tabs   You can change the margins and tab settings easily in Windows.

1. While in the Text Editor, click the **E**dit menu, the Text **E**ditor option, and then the Margins/**T**abs option from the submenu.

2. Fill in the Margins/Tabs dialog box with desired settings. Click OK.

Displaying the Ruler   To display the ruler in the Text Editor in Windows, click the **E**dit menu, the Text **E**ditor option, and then the **R**uler option from the submenu; or press the Ruler icon button.

e**N**d attaching

Location: Attach menu

Purpose: To indicate that you are finished attaching file items such as text notes, graphics files, or DOS files.

When you choose *eNd attaching* from the Attach menu, you return to the Send menu.

reQuest receipt

Location: Address menu

Purpose: To ask cc:Mail to notify you of when the recipient of your message opens and reads the message.

Use this option when you want to be sure that the person(s) received your message. You will receive a receipt message even if the person you send the message to deletes the message before reading it. If you are using cc:Mail Remote, system administrators can select an option that will return a receipt either on arrival in the Inbox or upon opening the message.

The receipt message is a text message that, when received into your Inbox, can be treated like any other message. It includes the date and time the person opened the message.

In cc:Mail for Windows, select the Receipt check box directly underneath the Subject line of the address information.

Return to main menu

Location: Address menu, Send menu

Purpose: To erase any addressing or attachments that may have been configured and return to the Main menu. Your addressing information will not be saved if you

return to the Main menu. You will be prompted to
confirm that you want to cancel the message.

 To erase the address message header and all the text
you may have written in cc:Mail for Windows, close the
current window by double-clicking on the window's
Close button (–) in the upper-left corner of the window.

Send message

Location: Send menu

Purpose: To send a message from your personal
workstation to the person(s) for whom it was addressed.
cc:Mail will not send the message unless it has been
addressed properly. You will receive an error message if
you do not address the message to at least one person.
Subject lines are optional, but the message must have at
least one destination listed on the "To:" line of the
message header.

Step by Step

To send a message in cc:Mail for DOS:

1. Highlight *Prepare new message* from the Main
    menu and press ENTER, or use power key *P*.

2. Use the Address menu to address the message
    according to the desired options.

3. Highlight *eNd addressing* and press ENTER or use
    power key *N*.

4. Fill in the subject line.

5. Type the text of the message in the blank text editor.

6. Press F10 to finish, and the Send menu will appear.

7. Select other options before sending the message, or highlight *Send message* and press ENTER (the "Send" option will not appear unless you have previously addressed the message). The Main menu will then appear.

 To send a message after creating and addressing the message in cc:Mail for Windows, click on the Send icon (which appears as a letter), or click on the **Message** pull-down menu and then click on Se**nd**.

You will then have to confirm that you want to send the message. Click "Yes" on the dialog box that appears. You will then see the dialog window again.

set Priority level

Location: Address menu

Purpose: To send messages as Urgent, Normal, or Low priority. Normal priority is the default for all messages. Urgent messages are sent first through the various cc:Mail post offices on the network. You may want to send large messages at low priority if there are other short messages that need to go first.

You can choose this option either before or after writing the message; however, you must use it before choosing *eNd addressing* on the Address menu.

Step by Step

To set message priority in cc:Mail for DOS:

1. Highlight *set Priority level* in the Address menu and press ENTER, or use power key *P*.

2. You will then be queried for a priority level and offered the choices Normal, Low, or Urgent. Press either N, L, or U and then press ENTER.

The assigned priority will appear underneath the "From:" line at the top of the screen. You only need to use the **N** option if you want to change your previous choice of **U** or **L**.

In cc:Mail for Windows, select the priority from the small drop-down menu directly underneath the "Subject:" line of the addressing information.

Chapter 3

Managing Your Mailbox

This chapter will discuss the following commands:

Add names to mailing list

add New title or select another

Change folder title

Change mailing list title

Change password

change Printer port

change printer Type

Change profile

create message Log

create Trash folder

Delete folder

Delete mailing list

Erase names from mailing list

manage Folders

manage Mailing lists

Return to main menu

View mail directory

View mailing list

These commands are found in the Folder, Mailing List, Manage, and Profile menus.

When you choose *Manage mailbox* from the Main menu, you can accomplish any one of seven operations:

- Add/Delete private mailing lists
- Add/Delete names from private mailing lists
- Add/Delete storage folders
- View the cc:Mail post office directory
- Change your cc:Mail configuration
- Create a "trash folder" to save deleted messages
- Create a message log for outgoing messages

When you change these items, you are configuring, or customizing, your own private settings in the cc:Mail database. The cc:Mail program on your computer will act the way you want it to according to the settings you select. Because the cc:Mail post office is on a network, you can start cc:Mail from any computer on the network and access the same configuration settings.

Refer to Appendix A, Figure A-3, for a screen map of how all *Manage mailbox* menus are related in the cc:Mail for DOS environment.

 In cc:Mail for Windows, managing your mailbox is much less structured. You can choose management options such as creating folders, adding names to mailing lists, and changing your password at any time, even when you are preparing a message. You never have to go back to a Main menu to begin the process.

<u>A</u>dd names to mailing list

Location: Mailing List menu

Purpose: To add more user names to a personal mailing list. Only the system administrator can add names to a public mailing list.

Step by Step

To add names to a mailing list in cc:Mail for DOS:

1. Highlight *Manage mailbox* in the Main menu and press ENTER, or use power key *M*.

2. When the Manage menu appears, highlight *manage Mailing lists* and press ENTER, or use power key **M**.

3. Highlight the selected mailing list and press ENTER, or type the name of the list at the top of the screen. The Mailing List menu will appear on the right side of the screen.

4. Highlight **Add** *names to mailing list* and press ENTER, or use power key **A**.

5. When the cc:Mail directory appears, highlight a name that you want to add to the selected list and press ENTER.

6. Repeat step 5 for as many names as you want to add to the mailing list.

➤ *Speed Tip:* If you and several coworkers routinely send mail to the same list of people, ask the cc:Mail system administrator to create a public mailing list with your list of people. The mailing list will be available for everyone to use. All public mailing lists are marked with a #.

 In cc:Mail for Windows, you can add names to mailing lists by using the pull-down menus or by clicking on a name in the directory and dragging the name to a private mailing list.

To add names to a mailing list in Windows:

1. Click on the Private Mailing List icon, or click on the **S**elect menu and choose the Pri**v**ate Mailing list option. If you haven't created any private mailing lists, the list will be empty.

2. If you need to create a new list, click on the **F**ile menu and select the **C**reate Private Mailing List option. Fill in the dialog box with the name of your

new mailing list, and press ENTER. You can continue
to add names of new mailing lists or click Done to
finish.

3. If you already have a collection of private mailing
    lists, double-click the name of the list to which you
    want to add names.

4. A window showing the title of your list will appear.
    If you are creating a list for the first time, this list
    will also be empty. Now click on the Directory icon
    to show a list of all cc:Mail users on the network.

5. You should now have three or four different
    windows in your screen. To see all the windows at
    once, click on the **W**indow menu and select the **Ti**le
    option. All the windows will evenly fill the screen,
    as shown here:

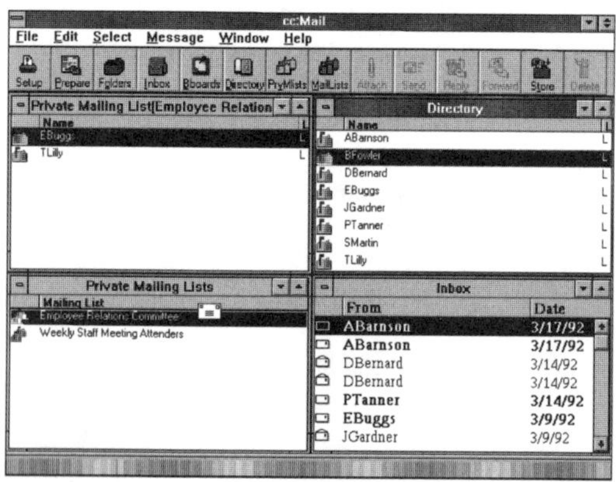

6. Click and drag one name at a time from the
    Directory window to your new mailing list window.
    As you drag names from the directory to your
    mailing list window, the names will appear in the
    order they appear in the directory.

➤ *Speed Tip:* Instead of dragging each name from the Directory to the mailing list, press the CTRL key as you click on each name you want to include. When all the names are highlighted, press the CTRL key and drag all the names at once to your new mailing list window.

add <u>N</u>ew title or select another

Location: Folder menu, Mailing List menu

Purpose: To add the name of a new folder or mailing list or edit the name of a folder or mailing list that already exists. Only the system administrator can add or change bulletin boards and public mailing lists.

Step by Step

To add or edit a folder or mailing list in cc:Mail for DOS:

1. Highlight *Manage mailbox* from the Main menu and press ENTER, or use power key *M*.

2. When the Manage menu appears, highlight either *manage Mailing lists* or *manage Folders* and press ENTER.

3. Highlight *add New title or select another* from the menu and press ENTER, or use power key *N*.

4. At the prompt, type the name of the new folder or mailing list you want to create or the name of a folder/mailing list that already exists. Press ENTER.

When creating the name of a folder, the program will show the name of the new folder on the screen. When creating a new mailing list, the program will immediately give you the opportunity to add names to the new list from the directory window.

 To add new mailing lists to your Private Mailing List in Windows, click on the Private Mailing List icon. When the Private Mailing List window appears, Click on the **F**ile menu and then click on the **C**reate Mailing List option. Fill out the dialog box and press ENTER. Add as many titles as you want and click Done to finish. The new mailing list will appear in the window.

To add names to the new mailing list, open the directory window. At this point, you might want to select the **W**indow menu and click on **T**ile to see all the windows at once. Click and drag names from the directory to the new mailing list. (See **Add names to mailing list** earlier in this chapter).

Change folder title

Location: Folder menu

Purpose: To rename a folder that you have already created.

Step by Step

To rename a folder in cc:Mail for DOS:

1. Highlight **Manage mailbox** from the Main menu and press ENTER, or use power key **M**.

2. Highlight **manage Folders** from the Manage menu and press ENTER, or use power key **F**.

3. When the list of folders appears on the right half of the screen, highlight the name of the folder you want to change and press ENTER.

4. When the Folder menu appears, highlight *Change folder title* and press ENTER (power key *C*).

5. Edit or replace the name of the folder at the prompt and press ENTER.

The new name will appear on the list of folders. All message items contained in the folder will still be there. Changing the name of the folder does not change the contents of the folder.

 To change the name of a folder in Windows, click on the Folders icon. When the window of folder names appears, click on the name of the folder (not the Folder icon to the left of the name). When the name is highlighted, you can edit the name of the folder as you wish. Press ENTER to complete the change.

<u>C</u>hange mailing list title

Location: Mailing List menu

Purpose: To rename a mailing list that already exists.

Step by Step

To rename a mailing list in cc:Mail for DOS:

1. Highlight *Manage mailbox* from the Main menu and press ENTER, or use power key *M*.

2. Highlight *manage **Mailing** lists* from the Manage menu and press ENTER, or use power key **M**.

3. When the list of mailing lists appears on the left half of the screen, highlight the name of the mailing list you want to change and press ENTER.

4. When the Mailing List menu appears, highlight *Change mailing list title* and press ENTER.

5. Edit or replace the name of the mailing list at the prompt and press ENTER.

The new name will appear on the list of mailing lists. All names in the mailing list will still be there. Changing the name of the mailing list does not change its contents. When you change names in the directory or delete them altogether, mailing lists will automatically reflect the changes.

To change the name of a mailing list in Windows, click on the Private Mailing List icon (you cannot change the name of a public mailing list). When the window of mailing list names appears, click on the name of the mailing list (not the Mailing List icon to the left of the name). When the name is highlighted, you can edit the name of the mailing list as you wish. Press ENTER to complete the change.

Change password

Location: Profile menu

Purpose: To change the password that you use to enter the cc:Mail program.

Step by Step

To change your password in cc:Mail for DOS:

1. Highlight *Manage mailbox* in the Main menu and press ENTER, or use power key *M*.

2. Highlight *Change profile* in the Manage menu and press ENTER, or use power key *C*.

3. Highlight *Change password* in the Profile menu and press ENTER, or use power key *C*.

4. Type your old password at the prompt and press ENTER. Then type the new password and press ENTER. The new password will be recorded in the cc:Mail database.

If the *Change password* option does not appear on the Profile menu, shown here, passwords are not required on the system.

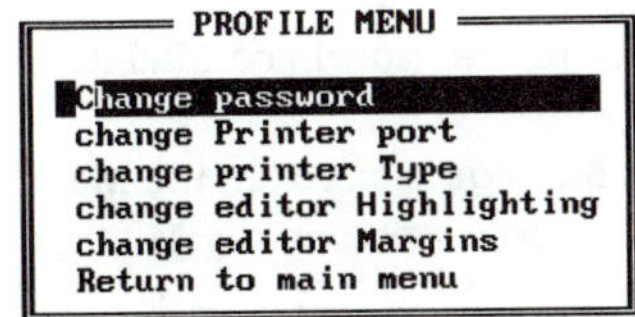

If you change your password, be sure to modify any .BAT files that may contain your password. Instead of typing the password every time, some users automate the login process by creating a .BAT file that automatically runs the normal command line instruction. Depending on your network and workstation configurations, this may not be a very secure way to log into the mail system.

Change your password in Windows by clicking on the **F**ile menu and choosing the Options menu selection. The first item that appears on the submenu is Change Password. Click on Change **P**assword and fill out the Change Password dialog box.

change **P**rinter port

Location: Profile menu

Purpose: To alter the port number (for example, LPT1, LPT2, LPT3) that cc:Mail uses to print documents from your computer. You might need to use this if your computer's LPT port is already configured to use a network printer, and you want to use a different network printer.

Step by Step

To change your printer port in cc:Mail for DOS:

1. Highlight *Manage mailbox* in the Main menu and press ENTER, or use power key *M*.

2. Highlight *Change profile* in the Manage menu and press ENTER, or use power key *C*.

3. Highlight *change **P**rinter port* in the Profile menu and press ENTER, or use power key *P*.

4. Use the arrow keys to select either LPT1, LPT2, LPT3, or "Po default" (post office default set by the system administrator), from the Printer Port menu.

To change the port assignment for print jobs while working in Windows, you must invoke the Windows

Print Manager. cc:Mail for Windows uses the printer driver that is already installed by the Windows system to print. Unfortunately, the cc:Mail Print Setup option does not employ the printer port selection buttons provided by Windows.

To change the printer port in Windows:

1. Use CTRL-ESC to view the Windows Task Manager and double-click on Program Manager, or click on the Program Manager window in the background if cc:Mail window is minimized.

2. Click on the Main program group, which contains the various management icons used by Windows.

3. Click on the Print Manager icon. You will see a window similar to the window used by the cc:Mail Printer Setup option.

4. Click on the Options pull-down menú, and select the Printer Setup option. In the Printers dialog box, click the **Connect** button. You will then see a box that lists the port assignments you can use.

change printer **T**ype

Location: Profile menu

Purpose: To select a printer driver interface to print messages and other documents from cc:Mail.

Step by Step

To change or select a printer driver in cc:Mail for DOS:

1. Highlight *Manage mailbox* in the Main menu and press ENTER, or use power key *M*.

2. Highlight *Change profile* in the Manage menu and press ENTER, or use power key *C*.

3. Highlight *change printer Type* in the Profile menu and press ENTER, or use power key *T*.

4. Highlight the appropriate selection for your type of printer and press ENTER. When in doubt, ask your system administrator. He or she may have already set the post office default. The two HP Laser settings represent the standard 150 dots per inch (dpi) setting or a finer resolution 300 dpi setting.

 To change the type of printer used by your computer, use the Windows Print Manager as explained in *change Printer port*.

Change profile

Location: Manage menu

Purpose: To view or edit your password, printer port, printer type, default margins in the text editor, and text-highlighting defaults.

Step by Step

To change profile options in cc:Mail for DOS:

1. Highlight *Manage mailbox* from the Main menu and press ENTER, or use power key *M*.

2. When the Manage menu appears, highlight *Change profile* and press ENTER, or use power key **C**. When you first select the *Change profile* option in the Manage menu, you will see all current profile settings in two columns at the top of the screen. Your current settings are listed in the left side of the window, and the post office defaults for your cc:Mail installation are in the right side of the window. Version 4.0 shows a third part to the Profile window that shows settings for Config File, Resource File, Color Set, and Editor Map.

3. To change a setting, highlight the option and press ENTER, or use the appropriate power key.

4. If all are satisfactory, highlight *Return to main menu* and press ENTER, use power key **R**, or press ESC to return to the Main menu.

```
══════════════════════ cc:Mail Profile ══════════════════════
 Name: TLilly                       Post office: Acme-HQ
 Password: [        ]               PO Defaults:
 Printer port: LPT1                   LPT1
 Printer type: hp Laserjet stand res  Text only
 Editor highlighting: PO Default      (▵▵▵▵)
 Editor margins: PO Default           (L: 11 R: 70)
──────────────────────────────────────────────────────────────
   Config File: C:\MAILROOT\CCMAIL\CCMAIL.INI
 Resource File: C:\MAILROOT\CCMAIL\ENGLISH.RI
     Color Set: VGAnew.pal
    Editor Map: DOSMAIL.KEY
```

create message Log

Location: Manage menu

Purpose: To create a special folder that will save a copy of all outgoing messages. This option is new to version 4.0. Before, you could manually create a Message Log folder, but this option creates the log file automatically.

Step by Step

To create a Message Log folder in cc:Mail for DOS:

1. Highlight *Manage mailbox* from the Main menu and press ENTER, or use power key *M*.

2. When the Manage menu appears, highlight *create message Log* and press ENTER, or use power key *L*. (This option only appears on the menu when Message Log does not already exist.)

3. Type in a name for the message log, or press ENTER to accept the default name Message Log.

To create a Message Log in cc:Mail for Windows:

1. Click on the **S**elect pull-down menu, and then click on the **Fo**lders option.

2. When the Folder List window appears, click on the **F**ile pull-down menu at the top of the screen and then click on the **C**reate Folder option.

3. The Create dialog box will appear with the cursor flashing in a blank line. Fill in the blank with the name "Message Log."

4. Click the Create button and the Message Log folder will appear on the Folder List window. Every message you send will automatically be saved in the Message Log folder.

create Trash folder

Location: Manage menu

Purpose: To store deleted messages in one place, in case you ever need to retrieve an old message. This option only appears on the Manage menu when the Trash Folder feature is enabled by the network administrator.

Step by Step

To create a Trash folder in cc:Mail for DOS:

1. Highlight *Manage mailbox* from the Main menu and press ENTER, or use power key *M*.

2. When the Manage menu appears, highlight *create Trash folder* and press ENTER, or use power key *T*.

3. The Trash folder will appear as a normal personal folder in your list of folders. View the messages in the Trash folder in the same way you would retrieve and view messages in other personal folders.

 The Trash Folder is not available in cc:Mail for Windows. Once you delete a message using the "garbage can" icon, you will not be able to retrieve it.

Delete folder

Location: Folder menu

Purpose: To erase a folder and all the messages it contains. The messages in an erased folder cannot be recovered.

Step by Step

To delete a folder and all of its messages in cc:Mail for
DOS:

1. Highlight *Manage mailbox* in the Main menu and
    press ENTER, or use power key *M*.

2. When the Manage menu appears, highlight *manage
    Folders* and press ENTER, or use power key *F*.

3. Highlight the name of the private folder you wish to
    delete and press ENTER. The Folder menu appears in
    the left part of the screen.

4. Highlight the *Delete folder* option and press ENTER,
    or use power key *D*.

5. At the prompt, press Y for yes if you want to delete
    the highlighted folder or N for no if you do not want
    to delete the highlighted folder.

 You can delete folders from cc:Mail for Windows very
quickly with two or three clicks of the mouse:

1. Click on the Folders icon, or click the **S**elect menu
    and then click the **Fo**lders option.

2. When the Folders list appears in a window,
    highlight the folder name you wish to delete by
    clicking the mouse or using the arrow keys.

3. Click on the Delete icon that appears on the icon
    bar, or press DEL on the keyboard. Depending on
    how you have configured your system, a
    confirmation dialog window might appear asking
    you to confirm that you want to delete the selected
    folder. Click OK or press ENTER.

➤ *Speed Tip:* The confirmation dialog boxes are used to
safeguard against accidentally deleting messages,

folders, or mailing lists that contain important information. If you are confident that you will not delete important information, you can save yourself extra steps by turning off one or all of the confirmation dialog boxes.

Click on the **File** menu, and then click on the Options menu selection at the bottom of the menu. You will then see a list of features that can be customized to your liking. Click on the **C**onfirmation option. In the dialog window that appears, click on each check box where you want to disable the appropriate confirmation dialog window, as shown here:

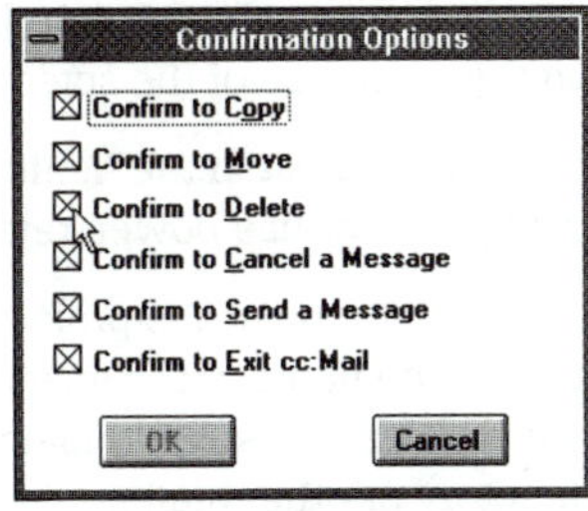

Delete mailing list

Location: Mailing List menu

Purpose: To erase a private mailing list.

Because a mailing list is only a subset list of names in the cc:Mail database, erasing a mailing list does not erase the names contained by the list. All names are preserved in the cc:Mail database; the names are "ungrouped," and the list name is deleted.

Step by Step

To delete a private mailing list in cc:Mail for DOS:

1. Highlight *Manage mailbox* in the Main menu and press ENTER, or use power key *M*.

2. When the Manage menu appears, highlight *manage Mailing lists* and press ENTER, or use power key *M*.

3. Highlight the selected mailing list and press ENTER, or type the name of the list at the top of the screen (you will only be able to delete the mailing lists that you created—only the cc:Mail administrator can delete public mailing lists). The Mailing List menu will appear on the right side of the screen.

4. Highlight *Delete mailing list* in the Mailing List menu and press ENTER, or use power key *D*.

5. Answer Y for yes or N for no at the prompt at the top of the screen. Only the name of the specified mailing list will be deleted. The users will remain listed in the cc:Mail directory or other mailing lists.

To delete private mailing lists in cc:Mail for Windows, click on the Mailing List icon and highlight the name of the mailing list you want to delete. Click on the Delete icon or press DEL on the keyboard.

Erase names from mailing list

Location: Mailing List menu

Purpose: To remove names from a customized list of users that you have previously created.

Step by Step

To remove names form a private mailing list in cc:Mail
for DOS:

1. Highlight *Manage mailbox* in the Main menu and
    press ENTER, or use power key *M*.

2. When the Manage menu appears, highlight *manage
    Mailing lists* and press ENTER, or use power key *M*.

3. Highlight the selected mailing list and press ENTER,
    or type the name of the list at the top of the screen.
    The Mailing List menu will appear on the right side
    of the screen.

4. Highlight *Erase names from mailing list* and press
    ENTER, or use power key *E*.

5. The names in your mailing list will be listed
    alphabetically at the top of the screen. Highlight
    each name you wish to erase from the mailing list
    and press ENTER.

6. Press ESC to return to the Mailing List menu.

 To erase names from a mailing list in cc:Mail for
Windows, click on the Mailing List icon from the icon
bar. When you click on the name of the mailing list, a
new window will appear with the title of the mailing list
at the top of the window. Highlight each name you wish
to erase and click on the Delete icon, or press DEL on the
keyboard.

manage Folders

Location: Manage menu

Purpose: To view, edit, create, or delete private storage folders. If you have not created any of your own folders, use this option only to view the list of bulletin boards (public folders) available to all users.

Step by Step

To create, view, edit, or delete private folders in cc:Mail for DOS:

1. Highlight *manage Folders* from the Main menu and press ENTER, or use power key *F*.

2. At the prompt line at the top of the screen, enter the name of the new folder you want to create, and press ENTER.

3. cc:Mail adds the name to the list of folders available to you (you are the only user on the network that can see the folder), and displays the Folder menu on the left half of the screen.

4. Use the Folder menu to change/delete the folder name or add a new folder name to your list.

 There is no menu selection in cc:Mail for Windows that opens the door to manage folders. You can create, edit, or change your private storage folders at any time by clicking on the Folders icon. Once the Folders window is open, select the **File** menu. Notice that the first three options allow you to open, create, or rename folders.

manage <u>M</u>ailing lists

Location: Manage menu

Purpose: To view, edit, create, or delete your list of private mailing lists. If you have not created your own mailing list, you can use this option to view the public mailing lists available to all cc:Mail users.

If you just want to view the names included on a particular mailing list, highlight the name of the public or private list and press ENTER. Notice how the Mailing List menu, shown here, allows all management options when a private mailing list is highlighted.

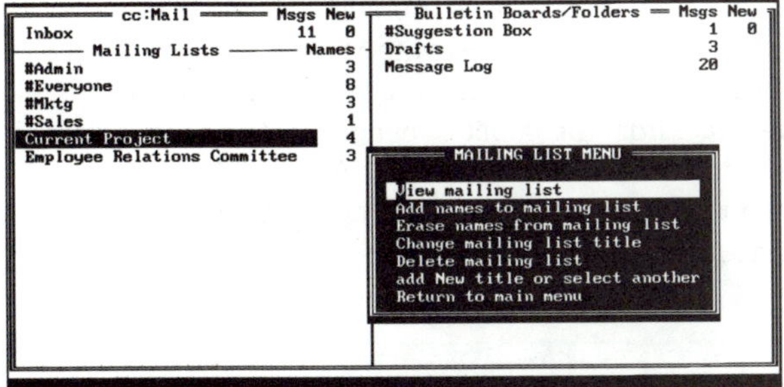

Step by Step

To create and then manage private mailing lists in cc:Mail for DOS:

1. Highlight *manage **Mailing** lists* from the Manage menu and press ENTER, or use power key **M**.

2. At the prompt line at the top of the screen, enter the name of the new mailing list you want to create and press ENTER.

3. cc:Mail adds the name to the list of mailing lists available to you (you are the only user on the network that can see the mailing lists you create), and displays the Mailing List menu on the right half of the screen.

4. Use the Mailing List menu to change/delete the mailing list name or add a new mailing list name to your list.

There is no menu selection in cc:Mail for Windows that opens the door to manage mailing lists. You can open, create, edit, or change your private mailing lists at any time by clicking on the Private Mailing List icon. Unlike the DOS product, private mailing lists in Windows are separate from the public mailing lists. Once the Private Mailing List window is open, select the **File** menu. The first three options allow you to open, create, or rename mailing lists.

<u>R</u>eturn to main menu

Location: Folder, Mailing List, Manage, and Profile menus

Purpose: To cancel all current operations and display the cc:Mail Main menu. You can also return to the Main menu by pressing ESC successive times until it appears.

<u>V</u>iew mail directory

Location: Manage menu

Purpose: To display the names of all the persons or external post offices that can receive and send cc:Mail messages via your electronic mail system. Others outside your system may also send messages via special add-on mail gateways. The directory also displays the date of last check-in for those labeled as locals (L), remotes (R), and comments inserted by the system administrator.

Step by Step

To view your mail directory in DOS:

1. Highlight *Manage mailbox* from the Main menu and press ENTER, or use power key *M*.

2. Highlight *View mail directory* and press ENTER, or use power key *V*.

Only the cc:Mail system administrator can add or delete names from this list. If your system's directory is very long, you can use the prompt line at the top of the screen to type the first few letters of the directory entry you wish to view. This saves having to use the PGDN and PGUP keys and/or the arrow keys.

To view the public directory in Windows, click on the Directory icon on the icon bar. You can have the Directory window open at any time while you are performing other tasks within cc:Mail.

View mailing list

Location: Mailing List menu

Purpose: To display all the names included in either a public or private mailing list.

Step by Step

To view a mailing list in cc:Mail for DOS:

1. Highlight *Manage mailbox* from the Main menu and press ENTER, or use power key *M*.

2. Highlight *manage Mailing lists* and press ENTER, or use power key *M*. The list of mailing lists appears on the left part of the screen.

3. Highlight either a public or private mailing list and press ENTER. The Mailing List menu appears on the right side of the screen.

4. Highlight *View mailing list* and press ENTER, or use power key *V*, and the list of users appears in alphabetical order at the top of the screen.

If you want to view the public mailing lists (marked with a #), you only have to highlight the mailing list and press ENTER.

To view the cc:Mail directory in Windows, click on the Directory icon, or use the **S**elect menu and click on the **D**irectory option.

Chapter 4

Reading and Managing Stored Messages

This chapter will discuss the following commands:

Act on messages	*search by **C**alendar date*
*reselect all **M**essages*	*search by **K**eyword phrase*
*retrieve from archi**V**e file*	*search by **P**erson*
*retrieve from bboard/**F**older*	*search by priority **L**evel*
*retrieve from **I**nbox*	*search for message n**U**mbers*
***R**eturn to main menu*	*search for **N**ew messages*
*scan message **H**eadings*	

These commands are found in the Retrieve menu.

The Main menu option *reTrieve messages* gives you the ability to search for and manipulate all messages that are stored in the your Inbox, bulletin boards, and folders. At times you might have to recall old messages in your folders or search for a particular message using cc:Mail's search-narrowing capabilities.

The idea behind retrieving messages in cc:Mail is to start with all messages selected, and then use the search and/or scan options on the Retrieve menu to narrow the group of selected messages until you find exactly the ones you need. When you find the right message(s), you can act on them as if you had selected them from your Inbox (see Chapter 1, "Reading Messages and Attachments"). To act on a group of messages, you will use the special Action menu used only for groups of messages.

Refer to the cc:Mail for DOS screen maps, Figure A-4, in Appendix A to see how all the menus fit together when you retrieve messages.

cc:Mail for Windows does not offer the structured Retrieve Message function of the DOS product. Stored messages (in folders, bulletin boards, Inbox, and archive files) are always available from the pull-down menus or SmartIcons. Even though there is a "Search" feature in cc:Mail for Windows, there is nothing in the Windows product that parallels the "narrowing" of a selected group of messages in the DOS product.

Once you have opened the window of messages in a storage folder, for example, you can use the **S**earch option from the **E**dit menu, or you can click on the Search icon to search text in the message header and in the Message text. The result of each search is a "Find Next" process. Once you have discovered one message with the desired text string, the program highlights the next message that fits the same criteria. The cc:Mail for Windows Search function does not group the messages that meet the search criteria, as does the DOS product.

The Windows Message Retrieval functionality is explained in this chapter where it relates to the DOS functionality. If you don't know which DOS menu selection to look under to find instructions for a specific Windows command, look in the comprehensive index at the back of the book.

<u>A</u>ct on messages

Location: Retrieve menu

Purpose: To read, copy, move, delete, write to disk, or print all the messages that are selected as a group. When you choose this option, an abbreviated Action menu, like the one shown here, appears with all available options. This is a special menu that only appears whenever you select *Act on messages* from the Retrieve menu.

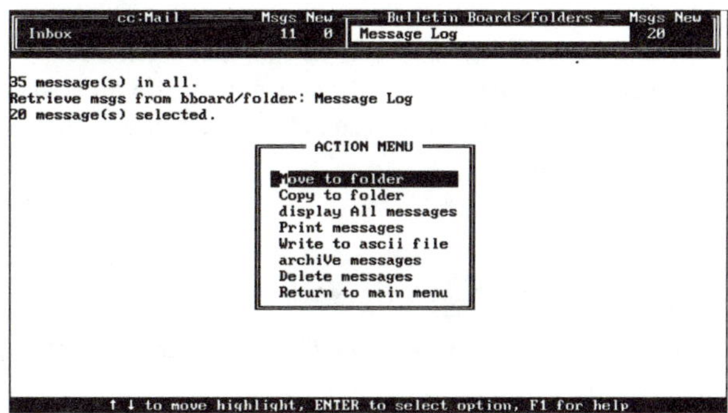

Step by Step

To act on a selected group of messages in cc:Mail for DOS:

1. Highlight *reTrieve messages* from the Main menu and press ENTER, or use power key *T*.

2. Notice how many messages are selected as noted above the Retrieve menu. If you want to perform any actions listed on the menu shown above, highlight *Act on messages* and press ENTER, or use power key *A*. You will be performing one of the

Action menu actions on the entire group of messages currently selected.

3. If you only want to perform actions on a smaller group of messages, use the other options on the Retrieve menu to narrow the selected group of messages before choosing *Act on messages.*

There is no Windows feature dedicated to "acting" on a group of messages. At any time you may select a group of messages using the SHIFT key as you click each one, and then perform a desired action by clicking on an icon from the icon bar, or by using the **M**essage menu at the top of the screen.

reselect all <u>M</u>essages

Location: Retrieve menu, after narrowing to a select group of messages

Purpose: To start the retrieving process over, as if you had just selected *reTrieve messages* from the Main menu. This allows you to reselect all messages. This option will appear if you have selected several messages, but the search cannot be narrowed further.

After you highlight *reselect all **M**essages* and press ENTER, or after you use power key *M*, the Retrieve menu appears with all available options, and you will see that all messages are selected as listed on screen above the Retrieve menu.

Since cc:Mail for Windows does not have a search capability like the DOS product, this option is not necessary in Windows.

retrieve from archi_V_e file

Location: Retrieve menu

Purpose: To select all the messages that were previously archived to a DOS file.

Once you identify the archive file, you will see the total number of messages on the screen above the Retrieve menu. If there is only one message in the archive file, that message will immediately appear on the screen, bypassing the Retrieve menu.

Step by Step

To retrieve messages from an archived file in cc:Mail for Windows:

1. Highlight *reTrieve messages* from the Main menu and press ENTER, or use power key *T*.

2. Highlight *retrieve from archiVe file* and press ENTER, or use power key *V*.

3. You will see the default path appear on the same line as the prompt. All files and subdirectories in that path are listed below the prompt line. Search for and highlight the archive file you want to retrieve by using the arrow keys, or change the file path by backspacing and typing the correct path. Once you highlight or type the correct archive filename, press ENTER.

4. Use the Retrieve menu to narrow the selected group of messages from the archive file, or use *scan message Headings* to look at each message.

Notice the path and name of the archive file listed above the Retrieve menu and listed in the bboard/folder window at the top of the screen. This is to remind you that the messages selected reside on disk, not in the cc:Mail database.

 In cc:Mail for Windows, there is no SmartIcon specially assigned to the archive store/retrieve process. You may use the Store SmartIcon to archive one or more messages, but to retrieve archive files you must use the pull-down menus.

To retrieve archive files in cc:Mail for Windows:

1. At any time in the program, click and open the **S**elect menu and click on the **A**rchives option. Unlike the DOS product, Windows remembers the DOS paths associated with each archive file.

2. When you see the list of archive files, click on the icon at the left margin of the desired archive file, or use the arrow keys to highlight the file and press ENTER.

3. When a new window opens with all the messages of the archive file, view or manipulate the message as you would with the Inbox. Click or press ENTER on the highlighted file to view the text of the message, or click on any one of the SmartIcons to perform the desired action.

You may also retrieve messages in Windows from an archive file that was created by the cc:Mail for DOS product as follows:

1. Click on the **S**elect menu and click on the **A**rchives option.

2. When the list of archive files appears in a new window, click the **F**ile menu and then click **C**reate Archive.

3. When the directory window appears, enter the path and name of the archive file created with the DOS product and press ENTER. The name of the archive file will now appear in your window list of archive files (provided you have rights to read the archive file).

retrieve from bboard/<u>F</u>older

Location: Retrieve menu

Purpose: To select one message or a group of messages stored in either a public bulletin board or a private folder.

After you choose one of the bulletin boards or folders listed in the window, you will see that the total number of messages selected equals the number of messages that are contained in the bulletin board or folder.

Step by Step

To retrieve a message from bulletin boards or folders in cc:Mail for DOS:

1. Highlight *reTrieve messages* on the Main menu and press ENTER, or use power key *T*. The total number of messages available for you to access is listed above the Retrieve menu.

2. When the Retrieve menu appears, highlight *retrieve from bboard/Folder* and press ENTER, or use power key *F*.

3. Highlight the title of the bulletin board or folder that you want to select and press ENTER, or type the title at the prompt line and press ENTER.

 To retrieve messages from bulletin boards or folders in cc:Mail for Windows:

1. At any time in the program, click on the Bulletin Board or Folder SmartIcon, or click and open the **S**elect menu and click on the **B**ulletin Boards or **F**olders option.

2. When you see the list of bulletin boards or folders, click on the icon at the left margin of the desired title, or use the arrow keys to highlight the title and press ENTER.

3. When a new window opens with all the messages of the bulletin board or folder, view or manipulate the message as you would with the Inbox. Click or press ENTER on the highlighted file to view the text of the message, or click on any one of the Smart-Icons to perform the desired action.

retrieve from Inbox

Location: Retrieve menu

Purpose: To select all the messages listed in your Inbox. Use this option to narrow the group of messages selected as noted on the screen above the Retrieve menu.

Step by Step

To retrieve messsages from your Inbox in cc:Mail for DOS:

1. Highlight *reTrieve messages* on the Main menu and press ENTER, or use power key *T*. The total number of messages available for you to access is listed above the Retrieve menu.

2. Highlight *retrieve from Inbox* and press ENTER, or use power key *I*. The Inbox will not appear on the screen. Instead, you will see the number of selected messages noted on the screen above the Retrieve menu.

3. Use the Retrieve menu options to further narrow the selected group of messages, or highlight *scan message Headings* to see all the messages in your Inbox.

If you choose to scan the message headings, you will then be able to highlight and select an individual message from your Inbox. When you select an individual message, the Action menu appears with options to read, forward, copy, move, and all other options that are available to you when you select *Read inbox messages* from the Main menu.

To retrieve Inbox messsages in cc:Mail for Windows:

1. At any time in the program, click on the Inbox Smart-Icon, or click and open the **S**elect menu and click on the Inbox option.

2. When you see the list of messages in the Inbox, click on the icon at the left margin of the desired message, or use the arrow keys to highlight the message and press ENTER.

Return to main menu

Location: Retrieve menu

Purpose: To cancel all operations and return to the Main menu. If you want to go back to the previous screen instead of going all the way back to the Main menu, press ESC once. You can also continue to press ESC at each screen to go back to the Main menu.

scan message Headings

Location: Retrieve menu

Purpose: To see all the message headings of the currently selected messages. The message headings will be listed on a screen similar to the Inbox.

Select this option from the Retrieve menu to narrow the group of selected messages either before or after you have used the other options on the Retrieve menu. If you choose *scan message Headings* from the Retrieve menu when all messages (from bulletin boards, folders, and the Inbox) are selected, you will see the message headings as they would appear in the Inbox, except they will be separated in sections according to where the message is stored. An example is shown here:

```
=================================== Inbox ===================================
   9 EBuggs              3/31/92   251t      Meeting on Wednesday
   4 ABarnson            3/20/92   170t      Meeting on Wednesday
   2 ABarnson            3/7/92    518t      Re: Q3 Forecast
   1 ABarnson            3/7/92    149t      Receipt of 3/7/92 11:13AM messa
============================= Folder: Message Log ============================
   4 To: DBernard        3/17/92   354t      Tee Time
   5 To: ABarnson        3/14/92   295t      Birthday Party for Eric
   9 To: ABarnson        3/22/92   288t      Review of our Products
  12 To: ABarnson        4/13/92   182t      Re: Receipt of 3/7/92 11:13AM m
  15 To: ABarnson        4/13/92   388t      Phone call to Johnson & Lauthie
  16 To: ABarnson        4/23/92   176t      new office supplies distributio
  17 To: ABarnson        4/26/92   378t      Proposal




  ↑ ↓ and ENTER to display message, F5 and F6 to select, Esc to end
```

After you scan the message headings, you can read and/or manipulate the messages as if you were reading messages in your Inbox by using the Action menu. The Action menu appears when you select a message from the Inbox. Refer to *Act on messages* in this chapter to know more about selecting a group of messages.

search by Calendar date

Location: Retrieve menu

Purpose: To select a group of messages according to the creation date listed on every message.

Step by Step

To select messages according to creation date in cc:Mail for DOS:

1. Highlight *reTrieve messages* on the Main menu and press ENTER, or use power key *T*. The total number of messages available for you to access is listed above the Retrieve menu.

2. Highlight *search by Calendar date* on the Retrieve menu and press ENTER, or use power key *C*.

3. Respond to the prompt "Search for msgs on or after date:" with a date in the form *MM/DD/YY* (such as 03/23/92) and press ENTER.

4. Respond to the prompt "Search for msgs on or before date:" with a date in the form *MM/DD/YY* and press ENTER.

➤ *Speed Tip:*   You do not have to fill in both dates after you select search on Calendar dates from the Retrieve menu. If you are searching for a message created before or after a certain date, and you don't care about pinpointing the exact date of a message, just fill in the date and press ENTER at one of the prompts and ignore the other one. For example, if you are searching for all messages related to a work project, and you know that all the messages were written before June 16, leave the "on or after" prompt empty, press ENTER, and then type **6/16/92** at the "on or before" prompt. You have now narrowed the number of selected messages to those created on or before June 16. Then select *scan message Headings* to look at the message headings.

cc:Mail for Windows does not support searching on creation or delivery dates.

search by Keyword phrase

Location: Retrieve menu

Purpose: To select a group of messages according to a word or phrase that appears in the subject, item titles, or full text of the message.

For example, if you want to retrieve all your messages relating to corporate finances, you would use this option to gather the messages from your Inbox, bulletin boards, or folders. You would then be able to perform one of several actions on this group of messages. You could print them, store them into one common folder, delete them, or perform other options that appear in the Action menu.

Step by Step

To select messages according to a word or phrase in
cc:Mail for DOS:

1. Highlight *reTrieve messages* on the Main menu and
    press ENTER, or use power key *T*. The total number
    of messages available for you to access is listed
    above the Retrieve menu.

2. Highlight *search by **K**eyword phrase* on the Retrieve
    menu and press ENTER, or use power key *K*.

3. At the prompt, type a word or phrase that appears
    in the message subjects and item titles (item titles
    applies to messages that have titles associated with
    attachments), and press ENTER.

4. In cc:Mail version 4.0 for DOS, you can search on the
    full text of the message. After entering the search
    string you will be prompted to indicate what text
    you want to include in the Search. Press *S* to search
    on subject lines and item titles only or press *F* to
    search on the full text of the messages.

5. When the Retrieve menu reappears, choose another
    option to narrow the group of messages further, or
    choose *scan message **H**eadings* to view the
    messages.

➤   *Speed Tip:* This option will be most useful if you fill in
the subject lines of your messages. It's a good idea to
get into the habit of being somewhat descriptive when
filling out the subject line. You might save yourself some
time later when you have to search for a specific
message.

cc:Mail for Windows supports searching in the text of
Messages, as in the DOS product. To search for a word

or phrase in the messages of the Inbox, a folder, a
bulletin board, or an archive file:

1. First click on the **S**elect menu and then click on
    either **In**box, **Fo**lders, **B**ulletin Boards, **A**rchives, or
    the appropriate SmartIcon.

2. If you select **In**box, you will see all the messages
    displayed. If you select **Fo**lders, **B**ulletin Boards, or
    Archives, you will see the list of titles. Click on the
    name of the folder bulletin board or archive you
    wish to search, or highlight the name with the
    arrow keys and press ENTER.

3. When the desired list of messages appears, click on
    the **E**dit menu and click on the Search option, or
    click on the Search SmartIcon that appears as a
    flashlight.

4. When the Search dialog box appears, as shown
    here, click on the desired combination of check
    boxes (**S**ubject, **F**rom, and/or **M**essage).

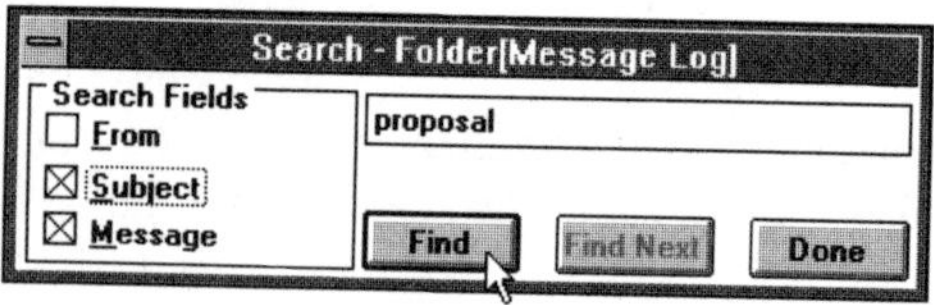

5. Click on the text prompt and fill in the text you wish
    to search for. Start the search by clicking on the Find
    button.

6. After one message is highlighted, click on the Find
    Next button as many times as there are messages
    that match the search criteria. Cancel the search
    whenever you want to view a message that
    matches the search.

search by Person

Location: Retrieve menu

Purpose: To search for a message or group of messages that were sent from or sent to one person. The person does not have to be the primary recipient of the message. This option will recover all messages where the selected name appears on a copy list, blind copy list, or on a mailing list.

Step by Step

To select messages by sender in cc:Mail for DOS:

1. Highlight *reTrieve messages* on the Main menu and press ENTER, or use power key *T*. The total number of messages available for you to access is listed above the Retrieve menu.

2. Highlight *search by Person* on the Retrieve menu and press ENTER, or use power key *P*.

3. You can type the mailing name of the person on the prompt line, or select the name from the directory list that automatically appears. You may only enter one name on the prompt line. The search is not case sensitive, so you can type the name without regard for capital letters.

4. When the Retrieve menu reappears, choose another option to narrow the group of messages further or choose *scan message Headings* to view the messages.

In any open list of messages (in a bulletin board, folder, Inbox, or archive file) in cc:Mail for Windows, you can click on the Search SmartIcon, or select the Search option from the Edit menu. Click on the check boxes (**F**rom, **S**ubject, or **M**essage) to search for a word or phrase in the message header or the text of the message. Fill in the search word/phrase. Click the Find button. Click the Find Next button to find the next occurrence. Click the Done button when you have located the desired message.

search by priority **L**evel

Location: Retrieve menu

Purpose: To search for a group of messages that all have the same priority level (Normal, Low, or Urgent).

Step by Step

To select messages by priority in cc:Mail for DOS:

1. Highlight *re**T**rieve messages* on the Main menu and press ENTER, or use power key *T*. The total number of messages available for you to access is listed above the Retrieve menu.

2. Highlight *search by priority **L**evel* on the Retrieve menu and press ENTER, or use power key *L*.

3. When the three options appear at the prompt line, press either *N* (normal), *L* (low), or *U* (urgent) for the group of messages you want to select.

4. When the Retrieve menu reappears, choose another option to narrow the group of messages further or choose *scan message **H**eadings* to view the messages.

cc:mail for Windows does not support searching for
messages with a certain priority level.

search for message nUmbers

Location: Retrieve menu, after narrowing to a select
group of messages

Purpose: To search for a message or group of messages
based on the number of the messages in the Inbox,
folder, or bulletin board.

There are two reasons why this search option is not very
effective: The order of the messages in an Inbox, folder,
or bulletin board can change, and message numbers
change when messages are deleted.

Step by Step

To select messages by message number in cc:Mail for
DOS:

1. Highlight *reTrieve messages* on the Main menu and
   press ENTER, or use power key *T*. The total number
   of messages available for you to access is listed
   above the Retrieve menu.

2. Highlight *search for message nUmbers* on the
   Retrieve menu and press ENTER, or use power key *U*.

3. Fill in the numbers of the desired messages,
   separated by commas. Press ENTER. You must have
   noticed the number of the desired messages prior to
   using this search option.

4. When the Retrieve menu reappears, choose another option to narrow the selected group of messages further or choose *scan message Headings* to view the messages.

search for <u>N</u>ew messages

Location: Retrieve menu, when there are new messages to be read

Purpose: To select all the messages in the Inbox, folder, bulletin board, or archive file that have not been opened yet. At times you will use this option after you have copied new messages to folders before reading them. You will also use this when you want to see all new messages at one time, even the ones in bulletin boards.

Step by Step

When you wish to retrieve new messages in cc:Mail for DOS:

1. Highlight *reTrieve messages* on the Main menu and press ENTER, or use power key *T*. The total number of new messages available for you to access is listed above the Retrieve menu.

2. Highlight *search for **N**ew messages* on the Retrieve menu and press ENTER, or use power key *N*.

3. When the Retrieve menu reappears, choose another option to narrow the group of new messages further, or choose *scan message Headings* to view the messages. When you view the new messages, you can treat them as if you were reading them in

the Inbox. Use the Action menu to save, store, or delete the message.

 To view new messages in cc:Mail for Windows, click on the Inbox SmartIcon or select **Inbox** from the **Select** menu. The new messages will be highlighted in a different color in the Inbox.

New messages may also be waiting for you in the public bulletin board folders.

Chapter 5

Special Features

This chapter discusses the following features:

Graphics Editor	cc:Mail Remote
TSRMail	Word Processor Key Mappings
Notify	Configuration File
Snapshot	Import/Export
cc:Fax	

cc:Mail offers several features to enhance electronic mail communications. Once you've established and worked with the cc:Mail post office at your local office, your cc:Mail administrator can add such things as fax capability and remote access for employees in the field. You may even be able to communicate with outside clients in other companies. Each of these features will be explained in this chapter.

Before the flexible add-on configurations, there are plenty of other bells and whistles available to you. Graphics, automatic notification, and screen capture utility programs offer a wide-range of possibilities for your day-to-day e-mail communications.

Graphics Editor

Location: Attach menu

Purpose: To create and edit graphical illustrations to attach to your mail messages. To use this feature, your

IBM PC or compatible must have VGA, EGA, or CGA video capabilities.

You do not have to use the cc:Mail Graphics Editor to send graphics file items with normal mail messages. You can send graphics files created from any drawing package via the cc:Mail system.

Step by Step

To begin illustrating with the Graphics Editor in cc:Mail for DOS:

1. Highlight *Prepare new messages* on the Main menu and press ENTER, or use power key *P*.

2. Address the message and fill in the Subject line according to regular Send Message instructions, as discussed in Chapter 2, "Sending Messages and Attachments."

3. Type the mail message in the Text Editor and press F10 to indicate that you are finished typing.

4. The Send menu appears in the middle of the screen, along with message header information at the top of the screen. Highlight *attach new iTems* and press ENTER, or use power key *T*.

5. When the Attach menu appears, highlight *attach Graphics item* and press ENTER, or use power key *G*. The graphics drawing screen immediately appears, with the menu information at the bottom and right sides of the screen, as shown here:

6. To turn the menu on and off, press F9; for help, press
    F1. Use appropriate drawing keystrokes (or the
    mouse) to create a drawing. The following list
    briefly describes the keystroke commands to use
    within the graphics utility:

Graphics Command	Keystroke
Help	F1
Display and Remove graphics menus	F9
Finish drawing, return to message	F10
Move the cursor around the drawing	Arrow keys
Select tool	Power keys, or move selection box around menus and press ENTER

Graphics Command	Keystroke
Freehand, thin lines	F
Freehand, thick lines	R
Empty circles	C
Solid circles	I
Empty boxes	B
Solid boxes	O
Straight line, thin	L
Straight line, thick	T
Small lettering	A
Large lettering	Z
Display spacing grid	G
Move a rectangular part of screen	M
Begin using selected tool	ENTER
End using selected tool	ENTER

7. Once you finish the drawing, press F10, and the graphic illustration will immediately be included on the Message Item list, along with the mail message you have already typed.

Users may also create graphics files with other graphics applications and attach those file to normal cc:Mail messages. The graphics file does not have to be created with the cc:Mail Graphics Editor to be included with a mail message.

The cc:Mail Graphics Editor does not exist in cc:Mail for Windows. Instead, cc:Mail for Windows employs the Windows Paintbrush application to create graphics images. See your Windows documentation for details on how to create graphics in Paintbrush.

TSRMail

Location: Loaded from the DOS command line and run from within any DOS application

Purpose: To automatically notify you of new messages in your Inbox while you are working in other applications on your workstation; to allow you to read and/or send messages while your other DOS application(s) remain active. TSRMail can only have a maximum of 16 users available in its memory-resident database.

Think of the TSRMail program (formerly Messenger in cc:Mail for DOS version 3.2 and prior) as exactly the same program as the normal Mail program, except that you can "hot key" in and out of TSRMail as you work in your other programs. After loading TSRMAIL.EXE, you will be advised when messages have arrived in your Inbox as in the Notify feature. TSRMail allows you to reply, send, read, and forward messages to others attached to your cc:Mail post office, all without exiting your current DOS application. TSRMail is a full-featured alternative to the regular Mail program.

Consider your computer's memory requirements when running TSRMail. Depending on the number of users on your system and the availability of expanded memory, TSRMail takes up anywhere from 4Kb to 18Kb:

	1 user*	**16 users**
No EMS available	11Kb	18Kb
EMS available	4Kb	11Kb

*1 *user's e-mail address in memory*

Step by Step

To use TSRMail from the DOS command line:

1. At the DOS command line, type **TSRMAIL** with appropriate command-line parameters, which are described in the next section.

2. Use the hot-key combination to view the list of new messages, or wait for the TSRMail screen to automatically appear on your screen. The default hot-key combination is ALT-2.

3. Highlight a message that you wish to read, forward, or reply to, and press ENTER.

4. When the Action menu appears, highlight the appropriate menu item and press ENTER, or use a power key. See Chapter 2, "Sending Messages and Attachments," for details.

5. Terminate the Action menu session, and you will return to the exact spot in the DOS application you were running before you started TSRMail.

➤ *Speed Tip:*   Do not run TSRMail as a DOS application in a Windows environment. TSRMail might create an unstable memory environment during regular Windows operations. cc:Mail for Windows is well worth the investment. cc:Mail for Windows includes a notify feature that allows you to activate the full cc:Mail program.

Optional TSRMail Command-Line Parameters   When you load TSRMail from the command line, you can include any of the following parameters (*m* represents the drive and directory where TSRMAIL.EXE resides):

Command	Example	Comments
/alt*x*	m:tsrmail /alt3	ALT-3 would be the new hot key used to see the Notify message from within any application
/awake	m:tsrmail /awake	Starts TSRMail after being suspended by /sleep
/chkonly	m:tsrmail /chkonly	Used to check the post office for new messages
/clear/*x*	m:tsrmail /clear/10	Sets the number of seconds the TSRMail window stays on the screen; 0 means you must press ESC to clear the TSRMail window
/name*x*	m:tsrmail /name\\ Joy Gardener	For security; eliminates the program prompt when entered name is missing or incorrect
/noems	m:tsrmail /noems	Configures TSRMail to not use expanded memory even if it is available
/nogr	m:tsrmail /nogr	Overrides color video adaptor; sets to monochrome
/noprompt	m:tsrmail /noprompt	For security; requires the user to give user name, password, and post office path on the command line. cc:Mail will not prompt for these items as usual
/mail/*cmd*	m:tsrmail /mail/fifo	If you run MAIL.EXE when TSRMail is loaded, this command string will be passed to the Mail program.*

*In the example, the Mail program will start up with its Inbox messages in "first in-first out" order.

Command	Example	Comments
/maxusers /x	m:tsrmail /maxusers/9	Specifies maximum number of users
/mono	m:tsrmail /mono	Forces TSRMail to start in monochrome (black & white) colors
/password	m:tsrmail /password	Forces TSRMail to prompt for a password when the user presses the hot key
/remind/ seconds	m:tsrmail/ remind/10	Flashes a window on screen telling the user how many unread messages are in the Inbox
/remove	m:tsrmail /remove	Removes TSRMail from memory; must have been the last TSR program loaded before this command
/sleep	m:tsrmail /sleep	Temporarily suspends TSRMail so that pressing the hot key will not start the program; users must type **tsrmail /awake** from the command line to restart the program. Useful when you temporarily need all available memory
/tempdir\ path	m:tsrmail /tempdir\ m:\ccmail\ temp	Uses the specified path for a temporary swap file
/timer/ minutes	m:tsrmail /timer/12	Checks for new messages every x number of minutes. The default value is 5 minutes

Command	Example	Comments
/tone	m: tsrmail /tone	Sets TSRMail to notify the user of new messages by tone only; eliminates the need to press ESC every time the reminder window appears
/window	m:tsrmail /window	Sets TSRMail to notify of messages with a window only, no sound

 There is no implementation of the TSRMail program in Windows. Because of the task-switching capabilities of the native Windows environment, a Notify feature such as the one explained in this chapter is sufficient. As a Windows user, you would see the Notify message on the screen and simply switch applications in Windows by using the ALT-TAB toggle combination or by invoking the Task Manager with CTRL-ESC.

Notify

Location: Loaded from the DOS command line and activated from within any DOS application

Purpose: To automatically advise you of one or more new messages in your Inbox.

You can load Notify for more than one user on any machine. For example, if an administrative assistant needs to check electronic mail for five office workers and NOTIFY.COM resides on drive m:, he can load Notify five times, one for each user name. The first user, however, must be loaded with a special "extended" parameter:

m:notify /NAnnie Farrell /Dm:\ccdata extended /Alt3

Additional users only need a normal Notify command line:

m:notify /NBlitz Krieg /Dm:\ccdata /Alt4

NOTIFY.COM is a memory-resident program (it takes about 27Kb of system memory) that pops up onto the screen, no matter which application you are running, to tell you that a message arrived for you in the cc:Mail post office. Notify does not allow you to respond or view the message from within the current DOS application, as TSRMail does.

Step by Step

To use Notify from the DOS command line:

1. Load NOTIFY.COM at the DOS command line with appropriate command-line parameters before starting cc:Mail. (You may need to ask your system administrator where NOTIFY.COM is located on the network.)

2. Press the Notify hot-key combination (ALT-2 is the default), from either the DOS command line or within a DOS application, to see if you have any new messages.

3. When the Notify box appears and advises you about new messages, press ESC to clear the box and return to your application.

Optional Notify Command-Line Parameters   When you type **m:NOTIFY** (*m* represents the drive and directory where NOTIFY.COM resides) on the DOS command line, you can follow it with any of the following parameters:

Command	Example	Comments
/altx	m:notify /alt3	ALT-3 would be the new hot key used to see the Notify /message from within any application
/chkonly	m:notify /chkonly	Used to check the post office for new messages; NOTIFY.COM will not stay resident in memory; use it as a one-time check
/clear/ *seconds*	m:notify /clear/15	Sets the number of seconds the Notify window will remain on the screen (range is 0 to 3600)
/headings	m:notify /chkonly headings	Used only with chkonly; displays a window with message headings as they appear in your Inbox
/mono	m:notify /mono	Specifies a monochrome monitor; all windows will be displayed in monochrome format
/n	m:notify /nJoe Smith	Avoids a separate prompt for the user name
/p	m:notify /psecret	Avoids a separate prompt for the user password
/remove	m:notify /remove	Removes the NOTIFY.EXE file from system memory

Command	Example	Comments
/timer/	m:notify /timer/5	Specifies how often Notify checks the post office in minutes database for new messages (range is 1 to 1440)
/tone	m:notify /tone	Changes the default method of notification from tone and window to just tone
/windows	m:notify /window	Changes the default method of notification from tone and window to window only

cc:Mail for Windows has a built-in Notify command that you choose to activate at installation time or in the Notify Options dialog box (choose **F**ile menu, then **O**ptions menu, and then **N**otify). You do not need to load a program before running Windows. You must make sure that the post office path specified in the Notify Options dialog box is correct. If the Notify program cannot access the database, you will see an error message on the screen, and Notify will not load.

Snapshot

Location: Loaded from the DOS command line and activated from within any DOS application

Purpose: To capture (save a picture of) an application's screen to send to another person. SNAPSHOT.COM saves the screen shot to a file. The recipient may then view the graphics file by using *display Items* on the Action menu without running the application that was used to create the screen shot.

You may often want to send a picture of a document or spreadsheet rather than duplicate the information in a regular mail message. By running SNAPSHOT.COM at the DOS command line, you can take a snapshot of a particular screen in a different application and send it to your colleague. Attached Snapshots can be viewed from within all cc:Mail platforms without loading SNAPSHOT.

Step by Step

To use Snapshot from the DOS command line:

1. At the DOS prompt, before loading any of your DOS applications, switch to the local or network drive where SNAPSHOT.COM is located (you may have to ask your network/cc:Mail administrator). For instance, type **CD M:\EMAIL\CCMAIL** to switch to the M:\EMAIL\CCMAIL directory path.

2. Type **SNAPSHOT** at the DOS command line (several optional command parameters are explained in the next section).

3. Load your DOS application as you normally do.

4. At any time in the program, call up the Snapshot program from memory by pressing ALT-1 (the default hot-key combination). You can change this hot-key assignment by using the /altx command-line parameter.

5. When the Snapshot menu appears, highlight *Take and store snapshot* and press ENTER, or use power key *T*.

6. You will then be prompted for a filename to save the screen shot graphics file under. Type the local or network directory path with the desired name of the file (for example, **screen01.123**), and press ENTER.

Snapshot will take a picture of the screen as it appears, without including the Snapshot menu that overlays the screen. Snapshot places a confirmation window in the upper-right corner of your screen to let you know that the file was saved successfully to the desired filename. If you do not name the file, cc:Mail gives the Snapshot file a default name. The first four letters are "SNAP", followed by "VGA", "EGA", "CGA", or "HGC". The three-number sequential extension begins with ".001". A sample Snapshot file might be named "SNAPVGA.001". If Snapshot doesn't prompt you for a filename, it has probably saved a file under a default filename.

➤ *Speed Tip:*   If you plan on using the Snapshot utility regularly, put the SNAPSHOT.COM command line into your PC's AUTOEXEC.BAT file. The software will load automatically, bypassing step 1 above. The Snapshot terminate-and-stay-resident (TSR) program only takes 27Kb of system memory.

Optional Snapshot Command-Line Parameters   Type any of the following parameters after the word "snapshot" at the DOS command line (*m* represents the drive and directory where SNAPSHOT.COM resides):

Command	Example	Comments
@*filename*	m:snapshot @sample.123	The @ key followed by a filename of a previously captured screen shot tells snapshot to display the graphics file on the screen
alt*x*	m:snapshot alts	User-assigned hot key; *x* can be any number, function key, or upper/lowercase letter

Command	Example	Comments
mono	m:snapshot mono	Indicates you are using a monochrome monitor
remove	m:snapshot remove	Removes the Snapshot TSR from system memory

Working with Existing Snapshot files

Besides capturing and saving screen shots, Snapshot allows you to view previously saved Snapshot files. The file is not in any graphics format, just the same ASCII character-based (or video mode-based) screen representation that you captured with Snapshot.

You can also save existing Snapshot files in an ASCII format by using the Action menu option *Write to ascii file.* You may then edit and incorporate the file into your message or other files.

 There is no Windows version of the SNAPSHOT.COM screen-capture utility. The only way to use the Snapshot utility in Windows is to load it into a DOS application window before loading a DOS application.

cc:Fax (add-on program)

Location: Address menu, if you have purchased and included the add-on cc:Fax software package

Purpose: To send and receive FAX transmissions from within your cc:Mail program.

This feature requires an added software package from cc:Mail called cc:Fax. If you don't have this feature installed, see your cc:Mail administrator. This could save you hours of standing in line waiting for the fax machine in your office.

Your system administrator can add fax numbers into the cc:Mail directory so that all users can automatically dial a commonly used fax number. You can then add a fax entry to your personal mailing list so that a message you send to others on your network can simultaneously be sent by fax to another location.

Step by Step

To fax within cc:Mail for DOS:

1. Prepare a message as usual.

2. When you address the message, from the directory highlight the target FAX post office name and press ENTER.

3. At the "To:" prompt, type the name, a space, and the string "FAX#" followed immediately by the telephone number. For example:

   Harold Marsh FAX#1-310-456-7899

4. Finish sending the message as usual.

cc:Mail Remote (add-on program)

Location: Remote computer not on the same network as your cc:Mail post office if you have purchased cc:Mail Remote

Purpose: To help traveling employees, or employees at home to access electronic mail services from a laptop or portable computer via a remote modem connection.

This feature also requires an added cc:Mail software package called cc:Mail Remote. Most features are the same, except that messages are stored in one place before being downloaded or uploaded to the central post office. The additional software is needed as an interface between the PC, the modem, and the cc:Mail software already loaded on your file server. Notice how the Main menu, shown here, is different for cc:Mail Remote.

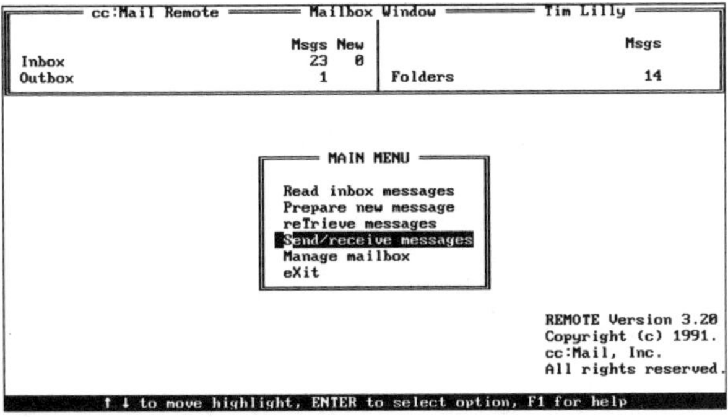

Remote allows anyone not physically connected to the LAN post office to connect to the post office to send and receive mail messages as long as the Post Office has cc:Mail Gateway or cc:Mail Dialin.

Most of the functionality is the same as in regular cc:Mail. However, there are specialized menus to handle the data communications part of sending messages to remote locations. Notice in the Send/Receive menu, shown here, how you can choose to dial the post office or send a message to a particular person.

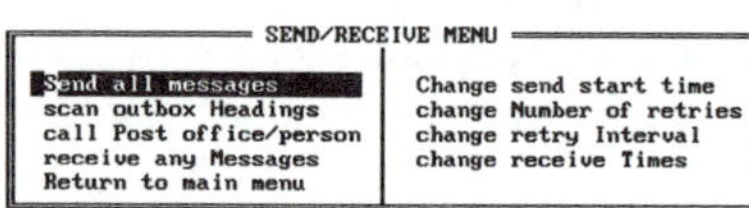

The Profile window, shown here, shows all of the settings you must configure in your cc:Mail Remote before it can communicate with the home post office. If your name is not entered here as it is at the home post office, you will not be able to receive the messages that your home office coworkers send to you.

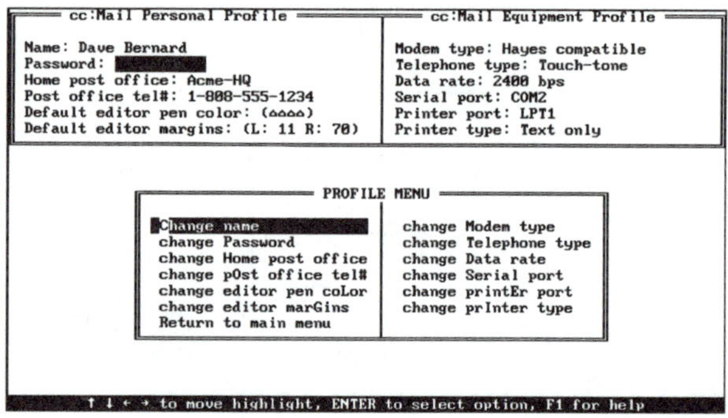

Word Processor Key Mappings (version 4.0)

Location: Configuration file

Purpose: To allow you to use the keystroke combinations available from other programs.

New in cc:Mail for DOS version 4.0, word processor key mappings allow you to replace cc:Mail's keystrokes with those that you might be more familiar with. You configure which type of word processor you want to emulate by changing your personal configuration file. Version 4.0 currently offers only two outside word processor keyboard mappings: AmiPro 2 (another product of Lotus), and WordPerfect. The cc:Mail for Windows keystroke set is also available to cc:Mail for DOS users. In the following segment of a sample configuration file (configuration file is discussed in the next section), note the names of the keyboard mapping files. The semicolon (;) indicates a remark line and tells cc:Mail to ignore this line of text. So, in this sample configuration file, the user will use the WordPerfect keyboard template:

```
[Mail]
;This statement defines the keyboard mapping
for the editor.
;Valid statements are DOSMAIL.KEY,
WINMAIL.KEY AMIPRO2.KEY
;and WPERFECT.KEY
;Keyboard Map=DOSMAIL.KEY
;Keyboard Map=WINMAIL.KEY
;Keyboard Map=AMIPRO2.KEY
Keyboard Map=WPERFECT.KEY
```

Note that this feature only replaces cc:Mail's keystrokes with the keystrokes of another word processor. The actual word processor functionality remains the same.

Configuration File (cc:Mail for DOS version 4.0 only)

Location: Viewed in Profile menu

Purpose: To set certain values and settings automatically.

The cc:Mail configuration file is new to cc:Mail for DOS version 4.0. The file sets important program parameters that makes using cc:Mail easier and more convenient. The configuration file is a DOS text file that can be created with any word processor, or even the DOS text editors EDLIN or EDIT.

After you have created the file with all the parameters that you want, you then must add an *environment variable* to your PC's memory (ask your system administrator or consult your DOS manual if you need help understanding environment variables). An environment variable is one of many internal settings that allows the operating system (DOS) or programs running on your PC to perform certain ways.

cc:Mail uses an environment variable as a pointer to the path where your configuration file is located. In other words, when the cc:Mail program first loads into your computer's memory, it looks for the configuration file. The environment variable tells cc:Mail where to find the configuration file. The name of the configuration file is your choice, but the name of the environment variable should be CCCONFIG.

Step by Step

To use a configuration file in cc:Mail for DOS version 4.0:

1. Create your configuration file according to the settings described at the bottom of this section.

2. Name the configuration file something that is easy to remember, such as "CCMAIL.CFG."

3. Enter the environment variable into your computer's memory by typing

   set ccconfig=c:\system\ccmail.cfg

   (Replace the location of the above file with the location of your configuration file.)

4. Start cc:Mail as normal either by using the MAIL.EXE program or the TSRMAIL.EXE program.

➤ ***Speed Tip:*** Place the "set ccconfig=" environment variable command in your system's AUTOEXEC.BAT or your CONFIG.SYS file so that it is automatically loaded every time you start your computer. Then you won't have to take time to type it every time you enter cc:Mail.

The configuration file has four main areas of settings:

[Common Parameters]
[Application Integration]
[Mail]
[TSRMail]

Fill in appropriate settings for your system according to the following example file. This file operates in the same manner as a Windows configuration file called WIN.INI. The settings categories do not have to be in any specific order:

```
[Common Parameters]
;This statement defines the color set to use
;Valid statements are VGANEW.PAL,
VGAOLD.PAL, MONONEW.PAL,
;MONOOLD.PAL
;Color Palette=VGAOLD.PAL
;Color Palette=VGANEW.PAL
;The next statement defines where to find
the resource file.
;Resource=ENGLISH.RI
```

```
;It can include a drive and a path also.
;Resource=d:\3german\german.ri

[Mail]
;The following statement tells the editor to
start in insert mode
Insert Mode=Insert
;The next statement defines the keystroke
mapping for the editor.
;Valid statements are DOSMAIL.KEY,
WINMAIL.KEY AMIPRO2.KEY and
;WPERFECT.KEY
;Keyboard Map=DOSMAIL.KEY
Keyboard Map=WINMAIL.KEY
;Keyboard Map=AMIPRO2.KEY
;Keyboard Map=WPERFECT.KEY
;Windows keystroke set was chosen above (no
; before statement)
;The next statement defines where to find
the dictionary file.
;It can include a drive and a path.
Main Dictionary=d:\mail\dexe\english.lex
;The next statement defines where to find
the personal dictionary
;file. It can include a drive and a path also
Personal Dictionary=d:\mail\dexe\user.lex
;The following statement defines some de-
fault command-line
;parameters for the mail program
Cmd= -N"Kevin Zerber"
;means that Kevin Zerber is the default post
office name: use -N or /N
;Cmd= /DM:\CCDATA
;means that cc:Mail database files are on
drive m: in CCDATA directory

[Application Integration]
;This section defines application-integration
bindings (binding
;an extension with a certain program)
;Next statement says to use EDIT for .TXT
```

```
files
TXT=edit.com ^
;Use BRIEF (B.EXE) for .C extensions
C=B.EXE ^.C [name=Brief Text Editor]
;Use BRIEF for .H extensions
H=B.EXE ^.H [name=Brief Text Editor (H
files)]
;DOC extension - use wordperfect (note use
of path)
DOC=D:\WP5\WP ^.DOC [name=WordPerfect 5.1]
;use BRIEF for .INI files
INI=B.EXE ^.INI
;use WORD for DOS for .WRD files (note use
of path)
WRD=D:\WORD\WORD ^.WRD [name=Microsoft Word
for DOS]
;use Ami Pro 2 for .SAM files
SAM=WIN ^.SAM [name=Lotus Ami Professional 2
for Windows]
```

cc:Mail for Windows does not use the same single configuration file as the DOS version. The functions of the cc:Mail for DOS version 4.0 configuration file already exist in many standard Windows features, including the WIN.INI file, which is the configuration file for Windows itself. For example, the association that might be TXT=edit.com ^ in the configuration file might be txt=notepad.exe^.txt in the WIN.INI file. Another standard Windows way to associate a file extension with a given program is through the standard Windows File Association dialog box.

Import/Export (add-on program)

Purpose: To import and export data into and out the cc:Mail post office database without using the normal menu-driven interface.

Import/Export is a DOS command line add-on product to the regular cc:Mail post office platform pack. It is mainly used by systems administrators and/or network administrators who need to duplicate directory lists or exchange mail data between programs. You will probably never have to use Import/Export in your daily work.

The program works by "exporting" names and data from the main post office to a regular text file. The text file has certain standard information like a "To:" line so the message can be sorted by destination, or other such data item.

After any sort of editing has been performed on the data, the data can then be "imported" by another post office or by the same post office. Types of files you can import and export include ASCII, DOS, FAX, and graphics files.

Chapter 6
Macintosh Quick Reference

Macintosh users can access and send messages through the same cc:Mail post office database as DOS, Windows, OS/2, and UNIX users. Network administrators can access the cc:Mail for DOS post office, for example, using the cc:Mail for Macintosh Admin program. The Mac Admin program also provides mail service for Macintosh-only networks. Regardless of how your network is set up, all of the cc:Mail features available to other users are also available to Macintosh users.

This chapter is arranged differently than the first five DOS/Windows chapters. In the Macintosh product, there are no structured menu steps. You can perform any function without starting at a "main menu." Therefore, each heading in this chapter represents a general task instead of a specific menu selection. This chapter will cover features for the new cc:Mail for Macintosh version 2.0. Previous versions are rather different that 2.0, so keep this in mind as you use this chapter.

Although the functionality maps in Appendix A are designed for the cc:Mail DOS product, you may find it helpful to review how all the cc:Mail functionality fits together. However, you will find the Graphical User Interface (GUI) of the Macintosh (or Windows) product is much easier to navigate than the DOS product. Most of the time you will start from the main cc:Mail window, where you can create messages, read messages, and find addresses and messages, as shown here:

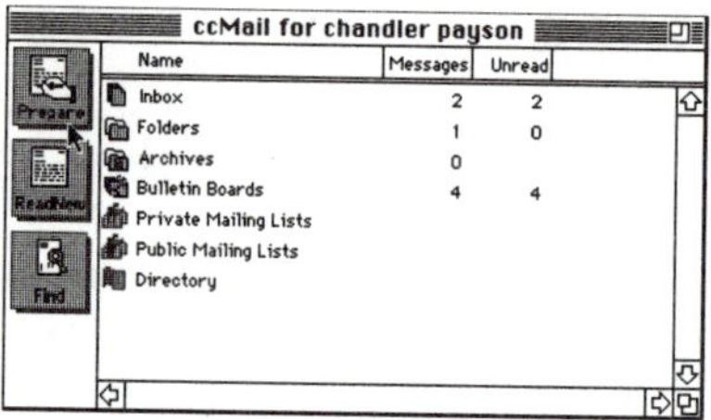

Attaching (Enclosing) File Items (text, graphics, sound, data)

You can easily include several types of resource files to enhance your electronic mail communications. When you attach a file item, you are only attaching a copy of the file. The file attachments appear in a small window "pane" in the regular message viewing or new message preparation window. Using the elevator bar to the right of the window, you can scroll up and down through the list of attachments. If you want to expand the attachment window, click and drag (move the mouse while holding the button down) the bottom border to a desired size and release the button. The message viewing window shrinks according to how large you extend the attachment window.

You can include text files, other text message items, sound files, PICT graphics files, or any other files produced with Mac applications.

Step by Step

To attach a file item to a cc:Mail for Macintosh message:

1. When preparing, forwarding, or replying to a
   message, click on the Attach icon at the top of the
   window, select Attach from the Message menu, or
   press ⌘-E.

2. When the Attach dialog window appears, navigate
   to the appropriate file volume or folder and highlight
   the desired file item.

3. Click the Attach button in the window or select
   Attach from the Message menu. You can repeat this
   procedure up to 20 times for each message you
   send. (You can send a maximum of 19 file items
   when you have text in the original message.)

If the file is not already created:

1. Click on the down arrowhead in the "Item Type:"
   box at the top of the Attach dialog window.

2. Choose the type of file you wish to include (for
   example, new sound, new PICT, or new text) and
   click the Create button, and the application will
   launch.

3. In the case of a sound file, you will see two buttons
   appear in the message portion of the window:
   Record and Play. If you press Record, you will see
   another dialog box, shown here, that lets you record
   an audible message (you must have the appropriate
   hardware installed on your Macintosh to create
   sound files).

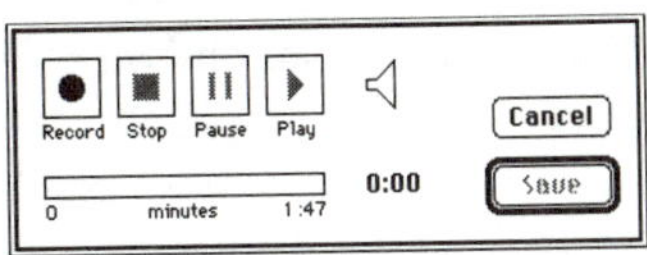

4. Click the Save button to finish recording the sound
   message and return to the Attach dialog window.

Your sound message will automatically be inserted into the list of attachments.

➤ *Speed Tip:* If you already have a hard disk volume or file folder open on the Macintosh desktop, you can click and drag the file item to the Attachment area in the cc:Mail window. You may find it convenient to resize your windows accordingly. You can also open other cc:Mail windows such as your list of messages within a storage folder, or your Inbox. Click and drag the desired text messages to the Attachment list.

Customizing User Settings (Preferences)

There are eight separate settings available that change such things as automatic return receipt, automatic save of outgoing messages in message log folder, reading most recent new messages, file mapping for launching applications, and text editor settings.

Step by Step

To change your cc:Mail for Macintosh user preferences:

1. At any point in the program, click the File menu and click the Preferences option.

2. Click the check box to set or remove each option:

Option	Description
Request Return Receipt	You can click on a Return Receipt check box each time you send a message, or you can click this check box to request a return receipt for every message you send.
Log Messages	Click this box to automatically save each message you send into a message log folder. (Your cc:Mail post office may not have this option enabled; check with your system administrator first.)
Remove Contents on Reply	Click this box if you want to delete the text of the original message from a reply message. You can deselect this option and include the original text with a reply message by clicking the check box that appears with each message.
Skip Trash Warnings	Click this box if you do not want to be warned before deleting messages or message items.
"Read New" reads most rec	You can change the order that new messages appear in your Inbox. Click this box to read the most recent new messages first (the "most recent" new messages means that you will not read the messages in chronological order).
File Mapping...	Starts a new dialog box that configures how other Macintosh applications are automatically started when you click on a certain file type.

Option	Description
Start Messages in:	Just as you might send a regular letter using a different process than another person, you can start creating your cc:Mail messages from different locations. Click the appropriate radio button to start sending a message from the "Subject:" line, the "To:" (Quick Addressing) line, the body of the message, or the Address window.
Text Editor...	Click this box to bring up another dialog box to configure your text editor. You can change the font, font size, text color, and background color of messages and then set up different colors for reply messages.

Customizing Lists of Messages, Names, and Folders

You can change several characteristics about each window that has a list, such as the Inbox, Folders, or Private Mailing Lists. Changeable items include the font of the text, the size of the text, and whether each column appears in the window.

Step by Step

To change how messages, names, or folders appear in a window:

1. While you are viewing a list such as your list of messages, list of folders, or list of mailing lists, click the File menu and click the Customize List option.

2. Click once on any of the scroll arrows that appear in fields representing the columns of the window or the font and size of the text in the window.

3. When the pop-up submenu appears, click on an option that changes that column or characteristic of the window.

4. Click Cancel to ignore your changes, or click OK to approve and save your changes.

To change the width of the column in a window, click on the divider lines in the heading until a separator icon appears at the cursor. Then drag the icon to the desired width. This method also works in windows such as the addressing window where there are three different subwindows.

Click, Drag, and Drop

cc:Mail for Macintosh has an advanced feature that allows you to click on a name, message, folder, or file item, and drag it so that it appears in another window. This makes working in cc:Mail windows easy and intuitive.

Step by Step

To drag one item with the mouse in cc:Mail for Macintosh:

1. Click on the item.

2. Hold the mouse button down while you drag the item across the screen to the destination window.

3. Release the mouse button.

To drag one or more nonconsecutive items:

1. Click and highlight the first item.

2. Move the cursor to the next item and hold down the SHIFT key while you click the next item. Both items should be highlighted.

3. Repeat this procedure for as many items on the list as you want to move.

4. When you have several items highlighted, hold down the SHIFT key while you click and drag *one* of the items. Notice how a shadow of all the selected items move as you drag the cursor to the destination.

5. Release the mouse button.

To drag consecutive items in a list:

1. Click and highlight the first item.

2. Hold down the ⌘ key while you click and highlight the last item. All the items in the list between the first and the last will be highlighted.

3. Hold down the ⌘ key while you drag one of the highlighted items to a destination window. All the highlighted items will follow if you keep the ⌘ key pressed while you drag the mouse cursor.

4. Release the mouse button.

There are many different situations where you can use dragging and dropping to save you time. You can drag and drop the following:

- A name from the Directory to the "To:" icon in the Address window

- A name from the Directory to the "cc:" (carbon copy) or "bcc:" (blind carbon copy) icon in the Address window

- A name from the Find window to the Address window

- A name from the Directory to a private mailing list

- A name from a private mailing list to the Address window

- A message from the Find window to a folder, bulletin board, or archive

- A message from the Inbox to a folder, bulletin board, or archive

- A folder to an archive file, bulletin board, or another folder

- A private mailing list to the Address window

- A public mailing list to the Address window

Finding Addresses

You can find a person's mailing address by typing the first few letters on the keyboard or by using the Find icon that appears in the main cc:Mail window (select Find from the Mail menu or press ⌘-F.

Step by Step

To find a person's address in the cc:Mail directory:

1. Enter the mail directory windows or a private mailing list window.

2. When the window appears and if you know the first few letters of the mailing address, start typing them at the keyboard. The highlight bar will immediately highlight the address entry that matches the letters you typed.

or

1. If you do not know the exact address, start at the main cc:Mail window and click the Find icon, or press ⌘-F.

2. When the Find dialog box appears, fill in the search script according to your search requirements. Click the down arrow of the submenu (drop-down list) that follows "Find all" and select "addresses".

3. Click the down arrow of the submenu that follows "whose" and select "name" or "comment" (you can identify an address by the text that appears in the comments field of the directory (for example, Vice President, Sales, or Tech Support).

4. In the next drop-down list, select "contains" if your search criteria is a partial search string (such as "presi" or "mar"), or select "is" if you know the whole address.

5. In the blank box that follows, type the search string that will identify the address(es) you want. You can use lowercase letters because the search is not case sensitive. The search line *does not* support wildcard characters such as * or ?.

6. Click the drop-down list that follows "Search:" and select "all addresses" or, if you are narrowing a search, select "found addresses" (you may also select either "inbox," "folders," "archives," or "bulletin boards").

7. Click on Find.

You can use the address(es) you find by clicking and dragging the address to the mailing list of a message you are creating, or to a private mailing list.

Finding Stored Messages

You can find a message by using the Find icon that appears in the main cc:Mail window. Search for a message based on the subject, message text, address, author, creation date, message size, priority, or names of file items.

Step by Step

To search for messages in cc:Mail for Macintosh:

1. Start at the main cc:Mail window and click the Find icon, select Find from the Mail menu, or press ⌘-F.

2. When the Find dialog box appears, as shown here, fill in the search script according to your search requirements. Click the down arrow of the submenu that follows "Find all" and select "messages."

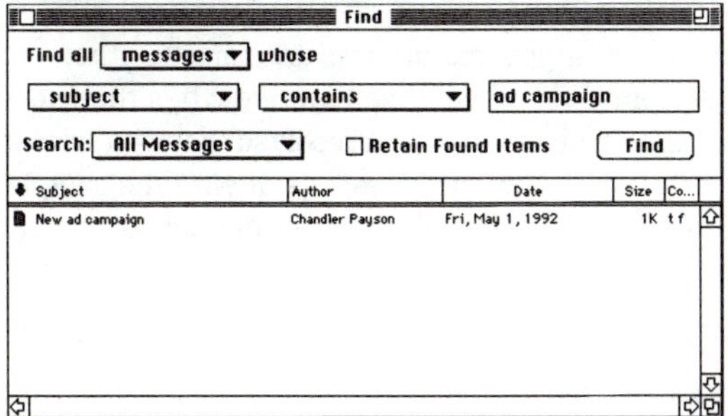

3. Click the down arrow of the drop-down list that follows "whose" and select "subject," "text," "address," "author," "data," "size," "priority," or "items."

4. In the next submenu, select the correct verb, based on which item you selected in the previous menu. For text, you would select "contains."

5. In the blank box that follows, type the search string that will identify the message(s) you want. You can use lowercase letters because the search is not case sensitive. The search line *does not* support wildcard characters such as * or ?.

6. Click the submenu that follows "Search:" and select "all messages" or if you are narrowing a search, select "found messages" (you may also select either "inbox," "folders," "archives," or "bulletin boards."

7. Click Find.

You can view and manipulate the messages you find just as if they were in your Inbox.

Forwarding Messages

Forward messages and/or message items to other people connected to your mail system when they need to see the same material you received. You can forward a message as a new mail message or with the complete forwarding history included in the address portion of the message.

Step by Step

To forward messages in cc:Mail for Macintosh:

1. When viewing a message, click the Forward icon at the top of the window, select Forward from the Message menu, or press ⌘-U.

2. Address the message as you would if it were a new message. Type names, choose names from the directory or a mailing list, or click on the Address icon. Type the subject line if desired.

3. Change the Priority, Log, or Receipt boxes if desired.

4. Edit the list of file items included.

5. If you do not want the recipient to know how many times the message has been forwarded, or if the forwarding history is irrelevant, click Forward as New from the Message menu. The message will be sent as if it originated from you. If you do not edit the message in any way, the heading reads "Forwarded". If you do edit the message but do not select Forward as New, the heading will read "Forwarded with changes".

6. Click the Send icon at the top of the window, choose Send from the Message menu, or press ⌘-D.

Launching Applications from cc:Mail

cc:Mail for Macintosh 2.0 takes advantage of the latest advances in the Macintosh System 7 operating system. You can only launch an application if you have System 7 installed on your Mac.

Launch or start an application just by clicking on an identifying filename. This is most often accomplished when someone sends you a message attachment that requires another application to view or edit the data file.

If the application resides on your hard disk volume or on the network, you can easily launch applications to view or edit attachments.

Step by Step

To start another Macintosh application from within cc:Mail:

1. Identify the file item you wish to view in the Attachments area of a message.

2. To launch an application associated with an item with the item loaded into it, hold down the OPTION key and double-click the file item icon, select Open from the File menu while holding down the OPTION key, or press OPTION-⌘-O.

3. If the Macintosh cannot find an application to run the selected file item, it presents a dialog box where you navigate to a desired disk volume to find an application.

4. If you change or edit the file in any way, cc:Mail will ask you to save the file under a different name. The file actually loaded into the launched application is only a copy of the original file item.

Preparing and Sending Messages

You can initiate message preparation from many different windows. For example, when you receive a message, you can reply to the message or forward the message with an entirely new message. The steps below assume you will be starting from the main cc:Mail window.

Step by Step

To send messages from the main cc:Mail window on
your Macintosh:

1. Click the Prepare icon, select Prepare Message from
   the Mail menu, or press ⌘-M.

2. Fill in the Addressing area, as shown here, by
   typing a name, dragging a name from the directory,
   or clicking the Address icon.

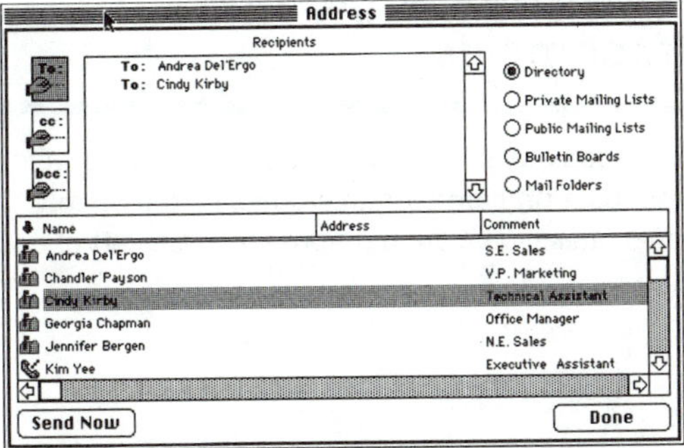

3. Click to the right of the Subject heading and type a
   subject. (Including a subject is optional; however,
   when you send the message and you do not include
   a subject, a dialog box will ask you if you want to
   send the message with or without the subject line
   filled in.)

4. Type the message text.

5. Attach any file items you wish to include.

6. Click on the Priority, Receipt, and Log boxes as
   desired.

7. Click on the Send icon, select Send Message from
   the Message menu, or press ⌘-D.

➤ *Speed Tip:*   If you routinely start using cc:Mail from the New Message window, you can configure cc:Mail for Macintosh to automatically open the New Message window whenever you open the program. Select Preferences from the File menu. Look for the "Start Message in:" section of the Preferences dialog box. Select Text Body from the list of starting options and click OK.

Reading Messages and Attachments

You can read any message that appears in your Inbox, a folder, a bulletin board, or an archive folder. Simply click the small message icon that appears to the left of each message.

Step by Step

To read only new messages in cc:Mail for Macintosh:

1. Click on the Read New icon from the main cc:Mail window, select Read New Messages from the Mail menu, or press ⌘-Y.

2. The first new message will automatically appear in the message viewing window, as shown here.

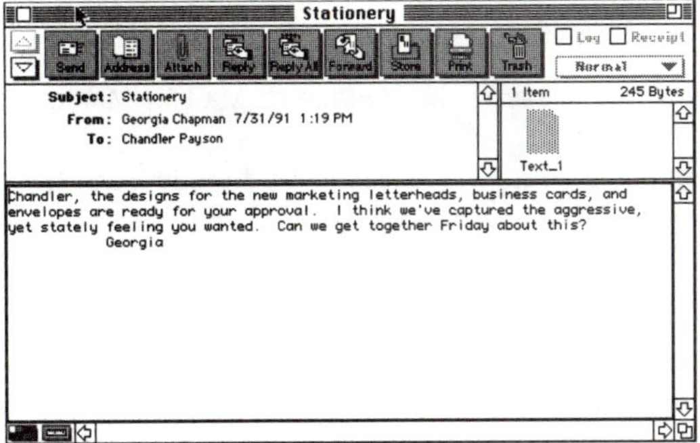

3. Click on the down arrowhead in the upper-left corner of the window to bring up the next new message.

To read all messages in the Inbox:

1. Click on the Inbox icon from the list of storage places and mailing lists in the main cc:Mail window.

2. Click on any one of the messages that appear in the Inbox, or highlight the message with the up and down arrow keys and press ENTER.

3. Click on the up arrow in the upper-left corner of the viewing window if you want to view the message that immediately precedes the current message in the Inbox. Click on the down arrow if you want to view the message that follows the current message.

Replying to Messages

You can reply to the individual who sent you the message, or you can reply to everyone that appears on the address list of the message. There is an icon available for each of these options.

Step by Step

To reply to messages received in cc:Mail for Macintosh:

1. While reading the message (or directly from the Inbox), click on the appropriate reply icon, select Reply from the Message menu, or press ⌘-R.

2. You will see the title of the window with "Reply to:" and the original subject line. The "Re:" tag will also appear in the subject line.

3. Enter your text anywhere in the message window. You can highlight the text (use the highlight icon at the bottom of the screen) or indent the text differently to differentiate it from the original message.

4. Click the Send icon, select Send from the Message menu, or press ⌘-D.

Storing Messages

Store messages in folders or archive files when your Inbox is getting too cluttered or if you wish to maintain a special collection of related materials. A *folder* in cc:Mail refers to the name of a storage location within the cc:Mail post office database, and is not to be confused with directory folders in Macintosh operating system software.

If the Message Log feature of the cc:Mail post office is enabled by your system administrator, you can automatically save a copy of every outgoing message in a message log folder.

Step by Step

To store messages in cc:Mail for Macintosh:

1. When reading a message, click the Store icon at the top of the window, select Store from the Message menu, or press ⌘-J.

2. Choose either the Mail Folders or Archives option at the bottom of the window. The window contents will change according to which option you select.

3. Click on the folder (or archive folder) in which the current message will be stored.

4. Repeat step 3 for archive folders.

5. To create a new folder or archive folder, open the list of folders and select New Folder from the File menu, or press ⌘-N. Type the name of the new folder and press ENTER.

➤ *Speed Tip:* If you wish to store messages directly from your Inbox, you can avoid reading the message and using the Store icon by clicking and dragging the message from your Inbox and dropping the icon on top of the name of the folder in your list of storage folders. You will have to open both windows from the main cc:Mail window to accomplish this procedure.

Using Mailing Lists

Mailing lists provide a quick way to send one message to a group of people without individually addressing the message for each person in the group. The system administrator creates public mailing lists for use by everyone on the network, and you can create private mailing lists for your use only.

Step by Step

To create a private mailing list:

1. From the main cc:Mail window, click on the Private
    Mailing list icon, select Private Mailing List from the
    Mail menu, or press ⌘-OPTION-P.

2. When the Private Mailing List window appears,
    select New Private Mailing List from the File menu
    or press ⌘-N.

3. Type the name of the mailing list in the space
    provided and press ENTER.

4. Click on the newly created mailing list to open the
    members list. Initially, there will not be anybody
    listed in the window.

5. Add names to the list by typing them yourself or by
    dragging and dropping the names from the
    directory, another mailing list, or an existing
    message with an address list.

➤ *Speed Tip:*   You do not have to open the new mailing
list to add names. You can click and drag names from the
directory and drop them on the new private mailing list
icon in the Private Mailing List window.

To use a private mailing list to address a message:

*   Open a private mailing list and click and drag the
    list to the "To:" line during message preparation.
or

*   From the Address menu, click on the Private Mailing
    list button and look at the list of mailing lists that ap-
    pear immediately below the Addressing portion of
    the window.

Chapter 7

Troubleshooting

This chapter covers technical tips and techniques that end users would use to solve common problems in cc:Mail. These troubleshooting topics are not exhaustive, nor are they written for the cc:Mail administrator who must set up and maintain the cc:Mail system on a local area network (LAN). The following tips describe problems end users might encounter during normal use. Each tip contains possible solutions and suggested courses of action. You will see that some problems will need the attention of your cc:Mail/LAN administrator.

Basic Troubleshooting Skills

The first basic rule of troubleshooting is to isolate the problem. Your odds of finding the problem are increased dramatically by eliminating parts of the system one by one. Most problems with LAN-based PC software can be traced to one of four areas:

- PC hardware
- PC software
- Network hardware
- Network software

Narrowing the possible reasons for trouble is the key to troubleshooting. There are many attributes of each category that help to narrow the focus of the problem. On the PC hardware, for example, you can look at the blinking lights on the computer to see if the power is on or the disk drives are working. In network software, you can see if you can send messages to a coworker at another workstation or if you can copy a file to the network server.

Troubleshooting Example

While in cc:Mail, if you experience a "File with that name cannot be created" error when trying to copy a message to disk, you might ask the following questions to narrow the search for the problem:

Is the file's destination my PC or the network?

From this question, you could eliminate two entire categories. If you are copying the file to your PC, you wouldn't concern yourself with the network hardware or software. Usually you can tell if you are copying to the network when your disk drive letter (A, B, C, etc.) is greater than D (F, G, H, etc.). Your next question might be

Is the file's destination my floppy or hard drive?

If the answer is "floppy," check your floppy disk drive to see that the disk is formatted and the drive door is closed. If those items check out, you might then check your hard disk drive to make sure you get a response when you look for files at the DOS command line. If it looks like the hardware is all working, check to see if there is enough room on the disk to which you want to copy, or that the directory to which you want to copy the file exists.

If, after all of these steps, you still can't determine what the problem is, you should probably give your system

administrator all the details of the steps you have taken
so far. Going through these troubleshooting steps will
help you to become more familiar with the computer and
will give the system administrator more information to
solve the problem faster.

You can solve many of the problems highlighted in this
chapter by becoming more familiar with cc:Mail
functionality. There are different troubleshooting steps
for every problem. But as long as you keep narrowing
the possible trouble spots, you are well on your way to
finding (and fixing) the problem.

Troubleshooting E-Mail Software Configuration

Problem

*Whenever I start cc:Mail for Windows, I get two
messages on the screen. One says "Can't open Database"
and the other says "Unsuccessful login, Try again?"*

Solution

There are two places where the e-mail software finds
out where the cc:Mail programs are located: the normal
DOS path command in your AUTOEXEC.BAT file, and
the WIN.INI file as part of your Windows system. In
DOS, use either the TYPE command, a text editor, or a
word processor to examine the contents of your
AUTOEXEC.BAT file.

 In Windows, check the "[CCMail]" section of the WIN.INI file to see if the information is correct. You can use the undocumented Windows SYSEDIT command if you want to see the SYSTEM.INI, WIN.INI, AUTOEXEC.BAT, and CONFIG.SYS files all at once. Click the File menu from the Windows Program Manager and click on Run. Type **sysedit** on the command line in the Run dialog box. You will then see four windows with the configuration files.

Problem

When I start my cc:Mail for DOS, I get a "bad command or file name" error message on the screen.

Solution

First check the correct spelling of the command. Then, from the DOS command line, try executing other network commands or switching to a network drive letter. If this is unsuccessful, the network may be disabled. Check with the system administrator. If the network commands are successful, your PATH command in your AUTOEXEC.BAT file may not contain the correct information. Change it yourself using a text editor or contact your system administrator.

Troubleshooting DOS Command-Line Parameters

Problem

*Whenever I type **Mail** to start cc:Mail, I get a "Bad command or file name" error message.*

Solution

This error indicates the computer cannot find the program to execute it. You must change to the network drive where the cc:Mail programs are located, or include the directory location of the files in your environment path. Ask your system administrator to help with either process.

Problem

It takes too long to fill in my name, post office, and password every time I start cc:Mail. Is there any way to speed up the process?

Solution

You can include all of these steps in one command line instruction. At the DOS prompt, type **mail** followed by your user name and the post office directory as follows (the forward slash in front of each parameter only applies to cc:Mail for DOS version 4.0):

mail /N"Sam Johnson" /Dm:\ccdata

All DOS versions earlier than 4.0 (3.21 and before) will appear without slashes, but must be in the following order:

mail *username password cc:Mail_data_drive*

for example,

mail Sam Johnson m:\ccdata

You can also include the password on the command line. Before adding the password to the command line, you should consider the security measures taken at your organization. When you add a password, the version 4.0 command line would look like this:

mail /N"TLilly" /Psecret /Dm:\ccdata

or, for version 3.21 and earlier,

mail TLilly secret m:\ccdata

Problem

After my network administrator upgraded our cc:Mail system to DOS version 4.0, I changed the old batch file that I use to start cc:Mail. The batch file doesn't seem to work anymore.

Solution

The old batch file should work because the new command-line syntax introduced in cc:Mail for DOS 4.0 is backward compatible. However, depending on the order of the parameters in the old batch file, you may have some problems. As long as you maintain the same batch file that you had in version 3.21 and before, the batch file should work fine. The main difference in the command line of version 4.0 is that you do not have to type each command-line parameter in a certain order. To let the program know what each parameter means, you have to precede each command with a forward slash (/) and a special character (D, N, P, etc.).

The following list shows all available command-line parameters with examples. If you don't enter the required information (name, password, or cc:Mail database location), the program will prompt you for the information before starting the program. Notice there is

no space in between the slash/letter combination and
the parameter.

/N"Jose Amigaso"

/Psecret

/Dm:\ccdata

All the other parameters used by TSRMail or Notify are
the same, except that you should now put a forward
slash in front of the command. For example, when
starting the Notify program, you might type the
following:

notify /N"Felix Unger" /Psecret /Dm:\ccdata /timer /Altx.

Command-line parameters are discussed in detail in
Chapter 5, "Special Features."

Problem

*I have a monochrome (two-color) monitor. Why does
cc:Mail look so unclear on the screen?*

Solution

If you have a color graphics adapter card installed inside
your computer, cc:Mail will detect the color adapter and
assume that you have a color monitor. If you have a
monochrome monitor, you should type **mono** at the
command line every time you start cc:Mail, along with
your user name, password, and post office directory. The
command line would look like this:

mail /N"TLilly" /Psecret /Dm:\ccdata /mono

Troubleshooting the Text Editor

Problem

Whenever I separate a paragraph into two paragraphs by pressing ENTER, the first line of the second paragraph gets cut off so it doesn't extend to the margin.

Solution

Use ALT-F8 to reformat the paragraph. All the lines in the paragraph will be filled in according to the default margin settings.

Problem

I can't use my BACKSPACE or DEL keys to delete a line from between two paragraphs.

Solution

Use ALT-F4 to delete an entire line in the Text Editor. You can also use the new cc:Mail for DOS 4.0 configuration file to replace cc:Mail's Text Editor keystrokes with the keystrokes of either WordPerfect or AmiPro. Other word processor keystroke commands will be available in the future.

Problem

Whenever I have been typing or adding text in the Text Editor for a while, I get a "Text Buffer Full" message. How can I add more to my message?

Solution

The cc:Mail Text Editor can only hold 20,000 characters
of data. To add more text to your message, you can
attach a text item to the original message. Choose
attach new iTem from the Send menu, and then choose
attach Text item from the Attach menu. In the new Text
Editor that appears, you can enter another 20,000
characters. After you are finished typing a new text
item, choose *eNd attaching* from the Attach menu, and
then choose *Send message* from the Send menu.

Problem

*I have already configured the cc:Mail Text Editor to use
a WordPerfect keyboard definition. When I import a
WordPerfect file into the cc:Mail Text Editor, there are
"garbage" characters at the top of the screen and all
throughout the message.*

Solution

The cc:Mail keyboard definition feature allows you to
change the keystroke definitions to the more familiar
word processor keystrokes, but it does not change the
cc:Mail Text Editor. The Editor can still only read true
DOS (ASCII) text files. To view the text you created in
WordPerfect in the cc:Mail Text Editor (the same holds
true for AmiPro), you must export the file or a portion of
it from WordPerfect to a DOS text file. You will then be
able to read the text file in cc:Mail's Text Editor.

Problem

*Whenever I press END to go to the end of the line in the
Text Editor, the cursor goes to the end of the message.
How can I move the cursor to the end of the line?*

Solution

Use the F3 key to go to the end or the beginning of the line. Try pressing F3 several times from the middle of a line of text. You will see that the cursor alternates going from the beginning to the end of the line.

Troubleshooting Message Reading

Problem

Whenever I look at the messages in my Inbox, I always have to scroll down to the bottom of the list to see the most recent messages. How can I make the most recent messages appear first on the list?

Solution

You can choose whether you want new messages to appear at the top or bottom of the list by adding a parameter on the DOS command line. The default cc:Mail setting places the new messages at the top of your Inbox list. By using a command-line parameter /FIFO (first in, first out), you can change the order of the messages in your Inbox so that the new messages appear last. If your program starts with the new messages last, your system administrator may have set it up that way on your machine.

To change the order in which your messages appear in your Windows Inbox, select Options from the **File** menu, and then select **Lists**. You may then choose between two display methods in your folders, bulletin boards, Inbox, and archive display windows. "Last in" will display the most recent message first, and "First in" will display the oldest message first. The default setting is "Last in" for the Inbox, folders, and bulletin boards. "First in" is the default setting for the archive windows.

Problem

I like to use as many SmartIcons as I can, but there is not enough room at the top of the screen to see all the icons.

Solution

You probably have the SmartIcons enlarged so that you can read the short text description included with each icon. After you become familiar with the icons you use the most, there are several ways to customize the icon bar. First, you can change the icon bar setting so that all the icons are the small size. More icons will be able to fit on the screen. Second, you can use the SmartIcons dialog box to customize the SmartIcon palette on your screen. Click on Options from the **F**ile menu and click on SmartIcons to see the dialog box.

Problem

I have trouble navigating the Action menu when I'm reading a message with several attachments. Whenever I try to move the arrow keys from one attachment number to the next, the cursor only moves on the Action menu.

Solution

To view and manipulate the file item attachments of a message, you must become familiar with three Action menu options:

- *List item titles*
- *display Items*
- *cHoose another item*

Use *List item titles* to see the subject lines or DOS file names of each of the attachments. Use the arrow keys when selecting an attachment from this list. When the number of a particular item is highlighted, use *display Items* to view it. Use *cHoose another item* to show the list of titles and select an attachment name to highlight. Press F10 to bring up the Action menu and then *display Items* to view it.

Troubleshooting Message Sending

Problem

Why doesn't the name of my private mailing lists appear on the "To mailing list" line of the address header?

Solution

Only the names of the public mailing lists (marked with a #) appear as mailing lists in the address header. Other people don't know about and cannot use your private mailing lists. Therefore, when you select a mailing list, only the names on the list are placed in the address header on the "To:" line.

Problem

I send large amounts of files to people every day. Why can I only send 19 file attachments to any one person? I

*thought I could send a maximum of 20 attached file
items in one mail message?*

Solution

You can send a total of 20 file items including the
original text item. If you need to send 20 attachments,
fill out the message header, but leave the mail message
blank. You will then be able to attach 20 file items.

Problem

I see the attach faX item *option on the Attach menu, but
how do I create a fax message to attach to my original
message?*

Solution

Your cc:Mail system administrator must add the cc:Fax
add-on product to your post office to be able to send and
receive faxes. The fax option on the Attach menu is used
to forward an electronic facsimile file that may have
come from another source.

Troubleshooting Your Mailbox Management

Problem

*If I want to get rid of messages in my Inbox, do I have to
mark each individual message with the* F5 *key?*

Solution

No! You can use F5 (begin block) and F6 (end block) to
mark an entire section of consecutive messages. You
may then move them all to a folder or delete them all at
once.

Problem

*I don't see a "Manage mailbox" equivalent in the cc:Mail
for Windows product. How do I change all my settings in
Windows?*

Solution

Most of the customizable settings in cc:Mail for
Windows appear as dialog boxes that you can choose
from the Options submenu. First, click on the **File** menu.
You will see the "Printer Setup..." option. Click on this
selection to see a Printer Setup dialog box. You will be
able to select one of the printers previously installed
using the Windows Print Manager. Select Options to see
other printer settings in a second dialog box.

To see the rest of the management settings, click on
Options on the **File** menu. On the submenu that appears,
you will see eight categories. After clicking any one of
the options, you will see an appropriate dialog box.

Appendix A
Screen Maps

The following Screen Maps represent a general flow of
control through the major features of cc:Mail for DOS.
These maps will help you become familiar with cc:Mail
very quickly. Please note that they are not intended to be
exhaustive and comprehensive; for more details on each
map's subject, see Chapters 1-4.

Figure A-1: Reading Messages and Attachments

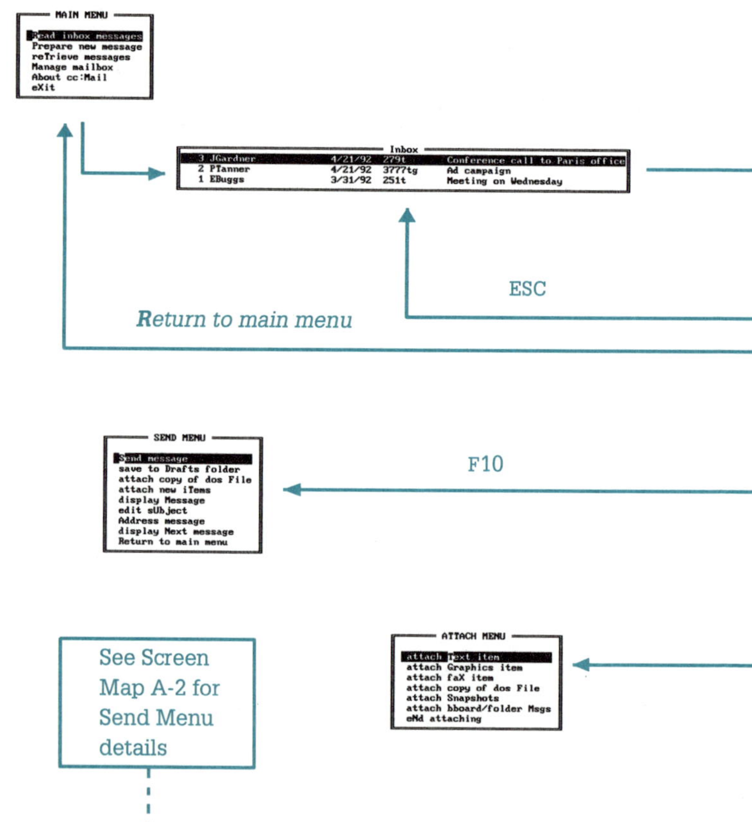

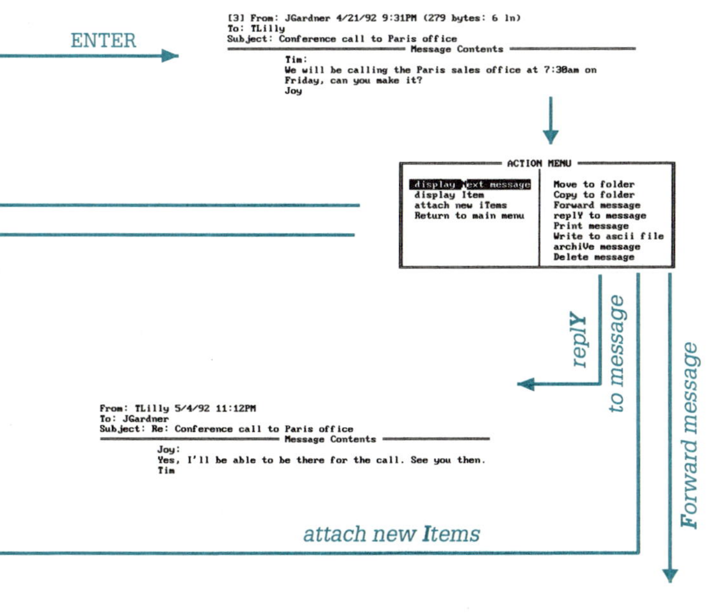
ENTER

[3] From: JGardner 4/21/92 9:31PM (279 bytes: 6 ln)
To: TLilly
Subject: Conference call to Paris office
————————————————— Message Contents —————————————————
Tim:
We will be calling the Paris sales office at 7:30am on
Friday, can you make it?
Joy

————————————————— ACTION MENU —————————————————
display next message   Move to folder
display Item   Copy to folder
attach new iTems   Forward message
Return to main menu   replY to message
                            Print message
                            Write to ascii file
                            archiVe message
                            Delete message

replY to message

Forward message

From: TLilly 5/4/92 11:12PM
To: JGardner
Subject: Re: Conference call to Paris office
————————————————— Message Contents —————————————————
Joy:
Yes, I'll be able to be there for the call. See you then.
Tim

attach new Items

————————————————— ADDRESS MENU —————————————————
Address to person   Copy to person
address to Mailing list   copy to mailing List
address to bboard/Folder   Blind copy to person
set Priority level   blInd copy to list
eNd addressing   reQuest receipt
Return to main menu

Figure A-2: Prepare New Message

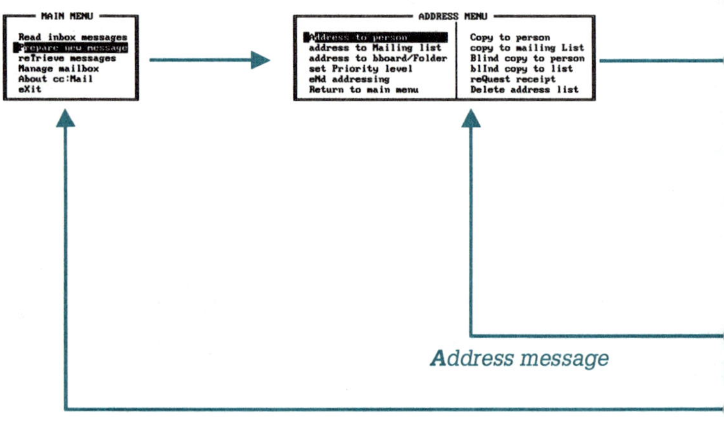

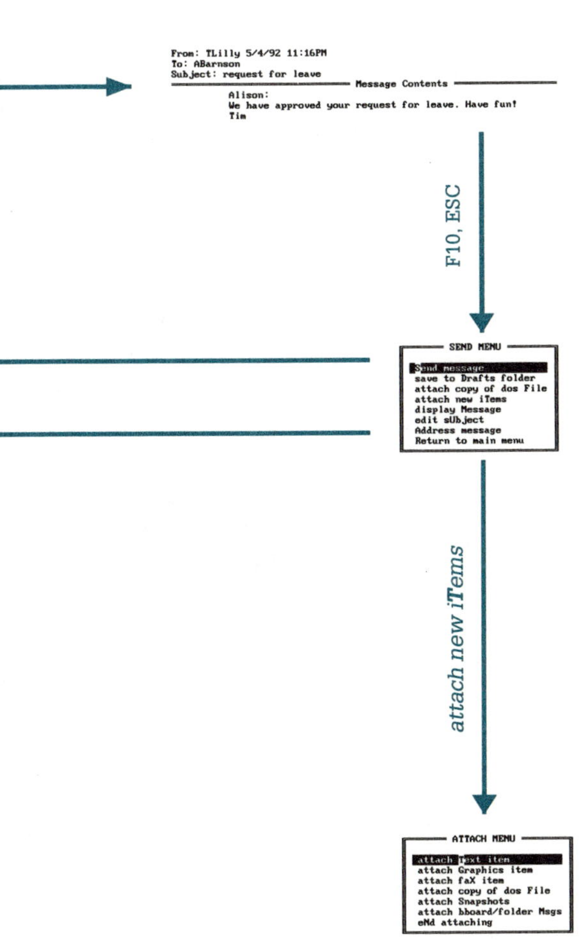
From: TLilly 5/4/92 11:16PM
To: ABarnson
Subject: request for leave
Message Contents
Alison:
We have approved your request for leave. Have fun!
Tim

F10, ESC

SEND MENU
Send message
save to Drafts folder
attach copy of dos File
attach new iTems
display Message
edit sUbject
Address message
Return to main menu

attach new iTems

ATTACH MENU
attach text item
attach Graphics item
attach faX item
attach copy of dos File
attach Snapshots
attach bboard/folder Msgs
eNd attaching

Figure A-3: Retrieve Messages

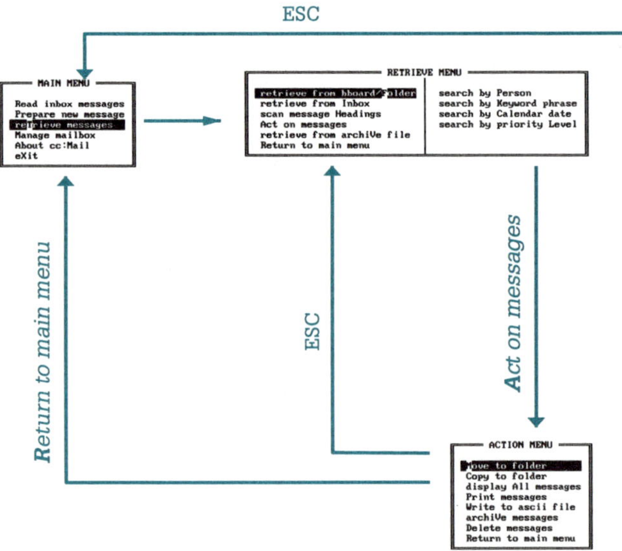

scan message

Headings

```
                                            ═══════ Inbox ═══════
       3  JGardner              4/21/92   279t       Conference call to Paris office
       2  PTanner               4/21/92   3777tg     Ad campaign
       1  EBuggs                3/31/92   251t       Meeting on Wednesday
                                ═══ Bulletin Board: #Suggestion Box ═══
       1  EBuggs                3/8/92    495t       Different Jobs
                                ═══════ Folder: Drafts ═══════
   D   1  To: PTanner           4/13/92   141t       new colors
   D   2  TLilly                4/21/92   258t       Proposal
   D   3  To: DBernard          4/21/92   173t       Letter for update package
   D   4  To: ABarnson          5/4/92    223t       request for leave
                                ═══════ Folder: Message Log ═══════
       1  To: PTanner           3/9/92    874t
       2  To: BFowler           3/9/92    225t       Weekly Staff Meeting
       3  To: DBernard          3/19/92   159t       Golf on Friday
       4  To: DBernard          3/17/92   354t       Tee Time
       5  To: ABarnson          3/14/92   295t       Birthday Party for Eric
       6  To: TLilly            3/14/92   191t       Golf on Friday
       7  To: TLilly            3/14/92   135t       Receipt of 3/9/92 8:42AM messag
       8  To: TLilly            3/8/92    489t       meeting with Johnson & Marlow
       9  To: ABarnson          3/22/92   288t       Review of our Products
      10  EBuggs                3/8/92    495t       Different Jobs
```

ENTER

```
[4] From: ABarnson 3/17/92 9:04PM (354 bytes: 7 ln)
To: DBernard, EBuggs, TLilly
Receipt Requested
Subject: Tee Time
════════════════ Message Contents ════════════════
    Guys-- I called Fair Oaks and got a tee time for Thursday
    afternoon at 4:24.  Alison.
```

ENTER

```
═══════════ ACTION MENU ═══════════
 display Next message   Move to folder
 display Item           Copy to folder
 attach new iTems       Forward message
 Return to main menu    replY to message
                        Print message
                        Write to ascii file
                        archiVe message
                        Delete message
```

See screen map A-2
for Action Menu details

Figure A-4: Manage Mailbox

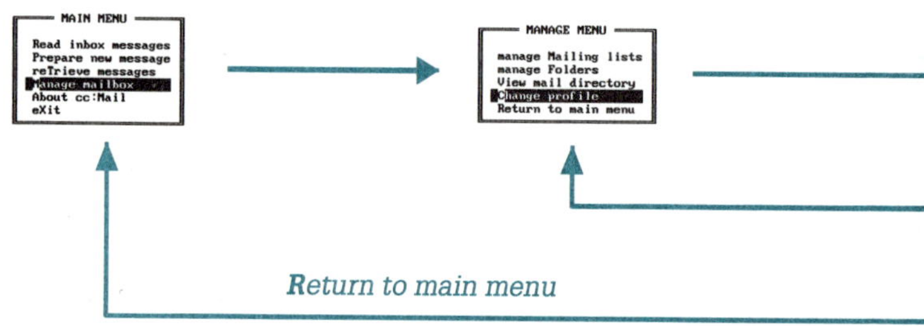

Return to main menu

*change **P**rinter port*

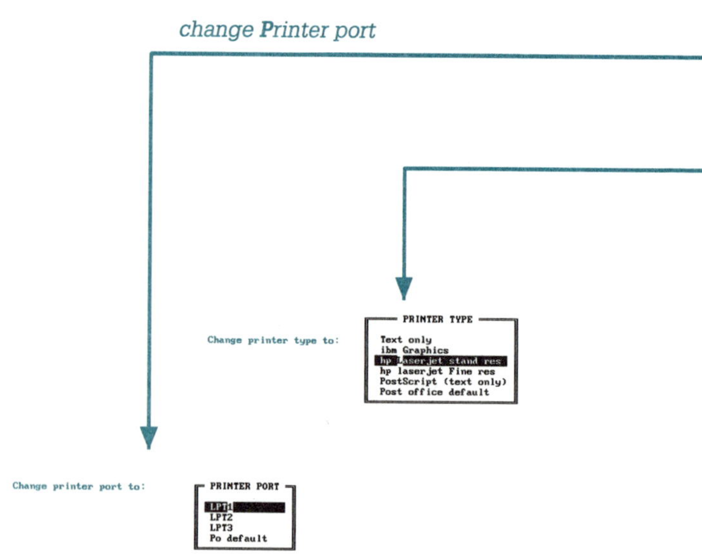

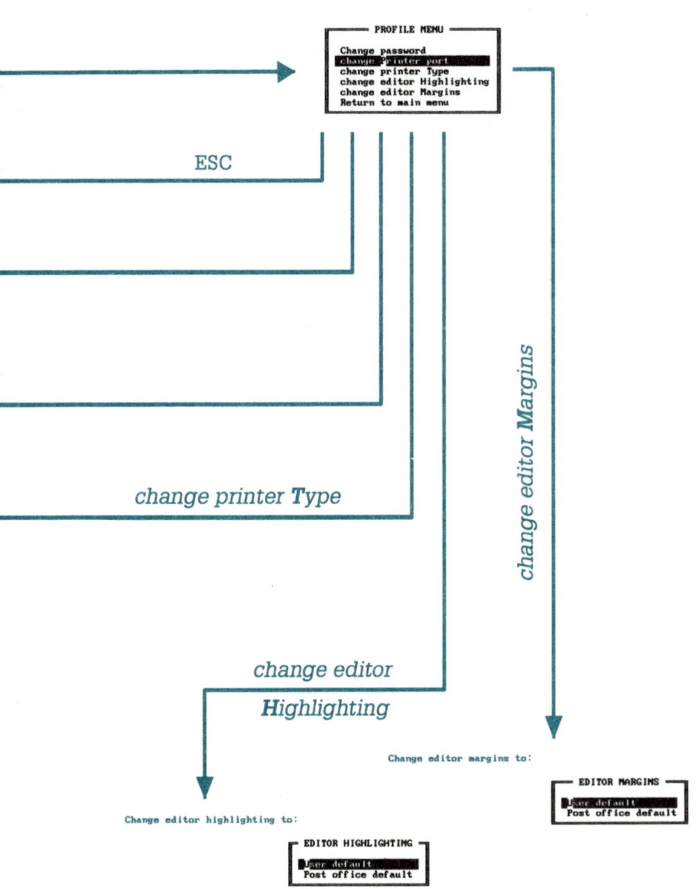
PROFILE MENU
Change password
change Printer port
change printer Type
change editor Highlighting
change editor Margins
Return to main menu
ESC
change printer Type
change editor Margins
change editor
Highlighting
Change editor margins to:
EDITOR MARGINS
User default
Post office default
Change editor highlighting to:
EDITOR HIGHLIGHTING
User default
Post office default

Appendix B
Keystroke Reference

cc:Mail for DOS

To accomplish any action outside the Text Editor, use
the appropriate menu commands as explained in
Chapters 1 through 4. Each menu command has an
equivalent power key, which, when pressed,
accomplishes the same thing as highlighting the
command and pressing ENTER. The power key is the
letter that is capitalized and bold in the command on
screen, for example the X in *eXit* on the Main menu. In
addition to commands executed by the power keys,
there are several functions that keypresses can perform
throughout cc:Mail for DOS:

Desired Action	Keypress
Move Highlight up, down, left, right one space	Arrow keys
Move Highlight to upper-left, upper-right, lower-left, lower-right corner	HOME, END, PGUP, PGDN
Select the option or end line of input	ENTER or F10
Return to previous without executing the command	ESC
Display a help screen	F1

For Graphics Editor keystrokes, see Chapter 2, "Sending
Messages and Attachments," under *attach Graphics
item*. When preparing, sending, or attaching file items to

messages, you can always use F10 to complete or ESC to abort the operation.

When Preparing a Message	**Press**
Cancel message	F10
Change margin settings	F4
Change screen colors	ALT-F1
Clear block markers	ESC
Copy a block (mark text with F5, F6)	ALT-F6
Delete a block (mark with F5, F6)	ALT-F4
Delete from cursor to end of line	ALT-F4
Delete search phrase (F7 to search)	ALT-F4
Edit mode (overwrites characters)	INS (toggle)
End editing	F10
Help	F1
Highlight block (use F5, F6)	ALT-F2
Highlight word	F2
Import DOS ASCII file	ALT-F9
Insert blank line	ALT-F3
Insert mode (moves characters to right of cursor)	INS (toggle)
Mark a single line as a block	F5
Mark beginning of block	F5
Mark end of block	F6
Move a block (mark text with F5, F6)	ALT-F8
Move to beginning of line	F3 once
Move to beginning of text	CTRL-HOME
Move to end of line	F3 twice
Move to end of text	CTRL-END

When Preparing a Message	**Press**
Move to next tab stop	TAB
Move to previous tab stop	SHIFT-TAB
Move to upper-left corner of screen	HOME
Print block (block with F5, F6)	F8
Print entire message	F8
Restore formatting (margins)	ALT-F8
Scroll text down one full screen	CTRL-PGDN
Scroll text down 1/2 screen (12 lines)	PGDN
Scroll text up one full screen	CTRL-PGUP
Scroll text up 1/2 screen (12 lines)	PGUP
Search and replace text	ALT-F7
Search for text	F7
Write to ASCII file (block with F5, F6)	F9

cc:Mail for Windows

In cc:Mail for Windows, the Power keys for commands
and menus are also single keys. You can recognize them
on screen by the letter that is underlined. In this book,
the power keys for Windows commands and menus are
in boldface, for example, the **O**ptions command in the
File menu. The power keys are discussed in the
Windows section (denoted by a small icon of a window)
of each command. Keypress combinations for cc:Mail for
Windows are shown here:

To Switch To	**Press**	**Menu**
Bulletin Boards window	ALT-B	Select
Directory window	ALT-D	Select

To Switch To	Press	Menu
Folders window	ALT-O	Select
Inbox window	ALT-I	Select
Mail Lists window	ALT-L	Select
Prepare Message window	ALT-P	Select
Private Mail Lists window	ALT-V	Select

To Change Window Arrangement	Press	Menu
Cascade	SHIFT-F5	Window
Tile	SHIFT-F4	Window

When Preparing New Messages	Press	Menu
Address message	ALT-A	Message
Attach file items	ALT-C	Message
Change margins/tabs	CTRL-T	Edit, Text Editor
Color Highlighting	CTRL-H	Edit, Text Editor
Copy	CTRL-INS	Edit
Cut	SHIFT-DEL	Edit
Delete	DEL	Edit
Paste	SHIFT-INS	Edit
Ruler	CTRL-R	Edit, Text Editor
Send message (after address)	ALT-N	Message
Undo	ALT-BACKSPACE	Edit
Use default margins	CTRL-D	Edit, Text Editor

To Act on Messages in Inbox	Press	Menu
Delete	ALT-DEL	Message
Store message(s)	ALT-T	File

When Reading a Message	Press	Menu
Delete message	ALT-DEL	Message
Forward message	ALT-R	Message
Reply to message	ALT-Y	Message
See next message in Inbox	ALT-RIGHT ARROW	Message
See previous message	ALT-LEFT ARROW	Message

cc:Mail for Macintosh

Although the Macintosh interface is largely graphics based and mouse oriented, there are keypress combinations that you can use to perform various tasks.

To Switch To	Press	Menu
Bulletin Boards window	COMMAND-OPTION-B	Mail
Directory window	COMMAND-OPTION-D	Mail
Folders window	COMMAND-OPTION-F	Mail
Inbox window	COMMAND-OPTION-I	Mail
Prepare message window	COMMAND-M	Mail
Private Mail Lists window	COMMAND-OPTION-P	Mail

To Switch To	Press	Menu
Public Mail Lists window	COMMAND-OPTION-M	Mail

When Preparing New Messages	Press	Menu
Address message	COMMAND-H	Message
Attach file items	COMMAND-E	Message
Clear	COMMAND-K	Edit
Copy	COMMAND-C	Edit
Cut	COMMAND-X	Edit
Delete	DEL	Edit
Highlighting	COMMAND-SHIFT-H	(none)
Launch external application	COMMAND-OPTION-O	(none)
Paste	COMMAND-V	Edit
Ruler	COMMAND-SHIFT-M	(none)
Send message (after address)	COMMAND-D	Message
Undo	COMMAND-Z	Edit

To Act on Messages in Inbox	Press	Menu
Delete message	COMMAND-DEL	(none)
Delete next message	COMMAND-OPTION-]	Message
Delete previous message	COMMAND-OPTION-[	Message
Find	COMMAND-F	Mail

When Reading a Message	Press	Menu
Delete message	COMMAND-DEL	(none)
Forward message	COMMAND-U	Message
Reply to message	COMMAND-R	Message
See next message in Inbox	COMMAND-]	Message
See previous message	COMMAND-[	Message
Store message	COMMAND-J	Message

Index

A

D

E

V

W